Ascending the
Mountain of
GOD

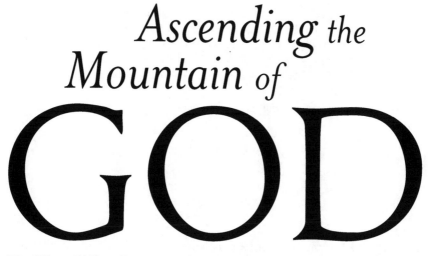

To Him Who Draws Nigh to God Must First Ascend

MATTHEW V. WHITE

WESTBOW®
PRESS
A DIVISION OF THOMAS NELSON
& ZONDERVAN

WestBow Press books may be ordered through booksellers or by contacting:

WestBow Press
A Division of Thomas Nelson & Zondervan
1663 Liberty Drive
Bloomington, IN 47403
www.westbowpress.com
1 (866) 928-1240

Because of the dynamic nature of the Internet, any web addresses or links contained
in this book may have changed since publication and may no longer be valid. The views
expressed in this work are solely those of the author and do not necessarily reflect the
views of the publisher, and the publisher hereby disclaims any responsibility for them.

All scripture quotations unless otherwise indicated are taken from the New American
Standard Bible®,Copyright © 1960, 1962, 1963, 1968, 1971, 1972, 19731975, 1977,
1995 by The Lockman Foundation Used by permission." (www.Lockman.org)

Any people depicted in stock imagery provided by Thinkstock are models,
and such images are being used for illustrative purposes only.
Certain stock imagery © Thinkstock.

ISBN: 978-1-4908-7339-8 (sc)
ISBN: 978-1-4908-7340-4 (e)

Library of Congress Control Number: 2015904151

Print information available on the last page.

WestBow Press rev. date: 04/23/2015

*To those
who hear His Call
and yearn to go higher.*

Contents

You have been called up the mountain of God and are seated with Christ in the heavenlies. Now answer the call and possess your inheritance in Christ.

To know God is to worship Him. To worship God is to give Him your all and your awe. Discover 7 ways to worship God that will release His presence in your life.

Mountaineering into the presence of God requires radical sacrifice. Evaluate 10 areas of life that compete for your allegiance to God and must be laid on the altar of sacrifice if you are going to be successful.

Throughout history God has demonstrated His nature and desire to communicate with His creation. Recognize the ways God speaks that will unlock His guidance for your life.

Procrastination and inactivity are obstacles that must be fought against as you ascend the mountain. Recognize how to fight against excuses that stall believers in the valley and keep them from the mountain top.

It is only through the supernatural revelation of God that you are able to discover your true identity: who you are in Christ, and your true purpose: who Christ is in you.

There is a standing invitation from God to ascend the mountain and enjoy Him in fellowship. What do you do if you're just not hungry? Learn 4 ways to increase your spiritual appetite for God.

Sometimes it seems the King of the Mountain is away. What do you do when your time on the mountain seems uneventful and empty? You learn the discipline of determined waiting.

God desires to impart to you supernatural wisdom so you can live the abundant life in Christ. Discover 7 ways to increase the wisdom of God in your life.

The mountain of God is a refuge for the burdened. Discover the supernatural rest for your soul that only Christ can provide.

Live every moment with passion, boldness, intensity, motivation and energy for God. How is this possible? Experience how to be filled with the Holy Spirit and fire!

The mountain dweller must prioritize and give up much for access on the mountain peak. What are you prepared to give up for face to face fellowship with the Father?

Exodus 24:1-18

Then He said to Moses, "Come up to the LORD, you and Aaron, Nadab and Abihu and seventy of the elders of Israel, and you shall worship at a distance. 2 "Moses alone, however, shall come near to the LORD, but they shall not come near, nor shall the people come up with him." 3 Then Moses came and recounted to the people all the words of the LORD and all the ordinances; and all the people answered with one voice and said, "All the words which the LORD has spoken we will do!" 4 Moses wrote down all the words of the LORD. Then he arose early in the morning, and built an altar at the foot of the mountain with twelve pillars for the twelve tribes of Israel. 5 He sent young men of the sons of Israel, and they offered burnt offerings and sacrificed young bulls as peace offerings to the LORD. 6 Moses took half of the blood and put it in basins, and the other half of the blood he sprinkled on the altar. 7 Then he took the book of the covenant and read it in the hearing of the people; and they said, "All that the LORD has spoken we will do, and we will be obedient!" 8 So Moses took the blood and sprinkled it on the people, and said, "Behold the blood of the covenant, which the LORD has made with you in accordance with all these words." 9 Then Moses went up with Aaron, Nadab and Abihu, and seventy of the elders of Israel, 10 and they saw the God of Israel; and under His feet there appeared to be a pavement of sapphire, as clear as the sky itself. 11 Yet He did not stretch out His hand against the nobles of the sons of Israel; and they saw God, and they ate and drank. 12 Now the LORD said to Moses, "Come up to Me on the mountain and remain there, and I will give you the stone tablets with the law and the commandment which I have written for their instruction." 13 So Moses arose with Joshua his servant, and Moses went up to the *mountain of God. 14 But to the elders he said, "Wait here for us until we return to you. And behold, Aaron and Hur are with you; whoever has a legal matter, let him approach them." 15 Then Moses went up to the mountain, and the cloud covered the mountain. 16 The glory of the LORD rested on Mount Sinai, and the cloud covered it for six days; and on the seventh day He called to Moses from the midst of the cloud. 17 And to the eyes of the sons of Israel the appearance of the glory of the LORD was like a consuming fire on the mountain top. 18 Moses entered the midst of the cloud as he went up to the mountain; and Moses was on the mountain forty days and forty nights.*

Unlocking the Summit

Who may ascend into the hill of the LORD? And who may stand in His holy place? He who has clean hands and a pure heart, Who has not lifted up his soul to falsehood And has not sworn deceitfully.

Psalms 24:3-4

Climbers speak of a mountain's "line", the route up its face that unlocks the summit. Before any great mountain is scaled, the successful climbers study this line and plan their ascent accordingly. In the twenty-forth chapter of Exodus, we see the line Moses climbed when God called him up to the top of the mountain.

Archeologists disagree as to the exact location of the mountain that God called Moses up and gave him the Ten Commandments. But one thing is certain, the Bible record is clear: God descended upon the mountain of Sinai, consuming its peak in an awesome demonstration of fire and smoke, trumpet blasts, and lightning and thunder that rattled the mountain, striking fear and terror in the hearts of the Israelites at the foot of the mountain. But Moses, so afraid his knees were knocking beneath his cloak, was emboldened by a personal invitation from God and he braved the mountain of Sinai, ascended the peak, and entered the Glory cloud. For forty days and nights he was engulfed by fire and smoke and surrounded by a cacophony of thunder and trumpet blasts, and his reward was the company of the Great I AM, the God of his forefathers Abraham, Isaac and Jacob.

Reading the Old Testament Exodus chapter twenty-four account of

Moses' ascent through a New Testament perspective, we begin to see a wonderful progression of intimacy with God as Moses climbed higher and higher and drew closer and closer to God All Mighty. Moses' climb physically up the mountain, culminating at its peak with a visitation from God is an example, a metaphor of God's purpose and invitation for you to climb spiritually up in Christ. In other words, in Exodus chapter twenty-four, we are given the "line" up the mountain, the map to His house, the key that unlocks the summit to His Holy Hill, the dwelling place of God!

You've Been Placed at the Foot of Mt. Zion

At the moment of your salvation, God rescued you from your old life; your sins that were leading you down a path of destruction and death and supernaturally placed you at the foot of a spiritual mountain. That mountain is referred to in the Scriptures by a variety of titles: the Hill of the Lord, His Holy Place, the City of the Living God, the Heavenly Jerusalem, and more specifically, Mt. Zion, and it represents the abiding presence of God in your life.

Just as God invited Moses up a physical mountain, Mt. Sinai, He now invites you up a spiritual mountain, Mt. Zion, to pursue Him in intimacy and fellowship. You were saved and placed at the foot of Mt. Zion and now God beckons you to climb. He is waiting for you to seek Him, to seek His face. And He promises if you will seek Him with all your heart and express your love and devotion to Him through faith and obedience, He will make himself known and come and make His dwelling within you. (Jn. 14:23; Jer. 29:13)

A Supernatural Mountain Awaits

The journey Moses traveled to the top of the mountain and culminating in face to face fellowship with God can be your mountain top encounter too. The invitation to intimacy is no longer reserved for prophets and privileged saints. Access to God has been granted for all who respond to His call. The author of Hebrews draws the parallel and significant difference between the journey of Moses up the physical Mt. Sinai and the journey of the believer up the spiritual mountain, Mt. Zion. Both the physical mountain and the spiritual mountain represent the pathway into the presence of God but from two very different perspectives.

Here is how Hebrews 12 describes the mountain Moses ascended:

> *For you have not come to a mountain that can be touched and to a blazing fire, and to darkness and gloom and whirlwind, and to the blast of a trumpet and the sound of words which sound was such that those who heard begged that no further word be spoken to them. For they could not bear the command, "IF EVEN A BEAST TOUCHES THE MOUNTAIN, IT WILL BE STONED." And so terrible was the sight, that Moses said, "I AM FULL OF FEAR and trembling."*
>
> *Hebrews 12:18-21*

This mountain is clearly the physical mountain Moses ascended to receive the Ten Commandments as recorded in Exodus. It was on this mountain the law was handed down from on High. Finally, man knew from the mouth of God what he had to do to earn the favor of God upon his life—to know God would accept him and not reject him in this life and the life to follow.

Mankind's Two Greatest Weaknesses

God's standard was clear and implicit: *"Be holy, because I am holy!"*. (Ex. 11:44) Instructions for a holy life were now in writing for all to follow. But what man discovered was that the law, the list of do's and do not's, was a heavy task master that demanded absolute perfection. He also realized that the law, rather than empowering him to holiness, instead inflamed his corrupt heart to rebel and resist! Rather than making him holy, and granting him access to a Holy God, the law exposed mankind's two greatest weaknesses. First, at the core of his being, his truest self, the law forced him to admit beyond contestation that his heart was corrupt and by nature evil. And the second fatal weakness the Law exposed in him was that because his heart was by nature evil and inclined to selfishness, in our his own strength and willpower he was powerless to master his inner pull to self autonomy. No matter how hard any person strived to live according to God's standard of righteousness, the only standard by which He approved and by which access to His Throne was made possible, they would eventually fail—everyone without exception.

Five hundred years of law abiding failures later, the Psalmist David penned his bitter conclusion: "*There is no one who does good.*". (Psa. 14:1) And his son, the wisest man who ever lived, Solomon, came to the same conclusion as his father: "*Indeed, there is not a righteous man on earth who continually does good and who never sins.*". (Eccles. 7:20) A thousand years later the Apostle Paul put it this way: "*for all have sinned and fall short of the glory of God,*". (Rom. 3:23)

> *Your mountain of destiny, is Mt. Zion, and it is a supernatural mountain that represents the dwelling place of God.*

Our nature was like a boat set to automatic pilot heading south and God demanded we go north. So we grabbed the steering wheel and working against its internal control to go south forced the wheel, turning the boat to head north by sheer will. As long as we gripped the wheel all was well, but eventually we grew weary or distracted and relaxed our grip, and true to its automatic pilot, the boat returned to its initial course, opposite of the preferred path.

The second fatal weakness the Law exposed in man was that in his own strength and willpower he was powerless to live according to the standard of righteousness, the only standard by which God approved and by which the only access to His Throne was made possible. No matter how hard he tried, and how he tried and believed he could be good enough, do good enough, all men eventually failed and fell short of the standard and glory of God required for holiness.

Ascending the Mountain of God

The sobering reality was on our own merit we were too weak and too prone to disobedience to make ourselves holy enough to be in the presence of God. For fifteen hundred years, from the giving of the law on Mt. Sinai until God gave His Son on Calvary, mankind continued to climb Mt. Sinai, to keep the law given to Moses and be justified before God by his works and obedience to the Law. But the bar of absolute perfection was too high. Mt. Sinai was a towering and foreboding mountain of works, and God sat at the top watching our every move. No man who attempted Mt. Sinai to justify his holiness by works made it to the top. He would eventually and assuredly transgress the law and fall, and no matter how long he lived and how many times he attempted, his obedience would eventually turn to disobedience, his cleanliness to uncleanliness, his righteousness to unrighteousness, and his holiness to corrupt sinfulness. Mt. Sinai stood before mankind beckoning him to ascend to its heights but strapped to his back was the law and it burdened the climber beyond all hopes of success. The law defeated even the very best climbers and sent them debased, demoralized and dejected back to the valley where the rest of sinful humanity lived.

But the Gospel declares God did not call you to Mt. Sinai! It is not the mountain you have been called to climb as Moses did. But you have been called to a mountain nevertheless:

> *But you have come to Mount Zion and to the city of the living God, the heavenly Jerusalem, and to myriads of angels, to the general assembly and church of the firstborn who are enrolled in heaven, and to God, the Judge of all, and to the spirits of the righteous made perfect, and to Jesus, the mediator of a new covenant, and to the sprinkled blood, which speaks better than the blood of Abel.*
> *Hebrews 12:18-29*

Your mountain of destiny is Mt. Zion, and it is a supernatural mountain that represents the dwelling place of God, where God can be

5

found and experienced. It is on Mt. Zion that even the angels look upon you in awe that you have been invited into a covenant relationship with the living God. It is on Mt. Zion that all those past and present who have believed in God have dwelt. It is on this mountain, the holy mountain of God, that you will find Jesus, the Savior of the world, who guarantees a better promise through the sprinkling of His own blood that offers the forgiveness of sins once and for all! It is upon this mountain, Mt. Zion, and only this mountain that relationship with Jesus can be possible. When you were saved you were placed on Mt. Zion and called to ascend!

The path up Mt. Sinai was paved with works, the path up Mt. Zion is hewn from grace. Mt. Sinai represented doing, and by contrast, Mt. Zion represents being. The invitation by God to ascend Mt. Sinai was destined for failure—the Law judged and condemned the heart of man guilty every time, but Mt. Zion represents not a Judge who condemns but a Justifier who saves. The focus of Mt. Sinai was on man's feeble attempts and inability to reconcile himself to God. The focus of Mt. Zion is on an all powerful God who sent His son to reconcile man once and for all and to do for man what he could not do for himself— that by the gift of God's grace and His righteousness, not of works, would make him holy that he may, unencumbered by sin, ascend to its pinnacle and enjoy the peace and presence of his Creator forever.

Which Mountain Are You Climbing?

It's very simple to know which mountain a person is climbing in their pursuit of God. If they think that good works will justify them before God and He will accept them on their own merit, then they are climbing Mt. Sinai. They have strapped to their back the burden of works and they will fail; the mountain is too high and the burdens of sin too heavy. But if a person pursues their Savior from a response to His gift of salvation by grace through faith—not their own works but by the works of Christ, God brings them to Himself through the life of His Son. This is possible because Jesus lived a sinless and perfect life and fulfilled the law, did for man what he could not do for himself, and died on a cross. Now His shed blood covers our sins and makes us holy and reconciles us, carries us to the peak of Mt. Zion, and into the presence of God. In other words, when a person stands upon the mountain top enjoying the presence of God and knowing it was God who seated them with Christ in the heavenlies, (Eph. 2:6) not because of anything they have done in and of themselves, then they are on the right mountain, Mt. Zion.

It is important that you ask yourself which mountain you are climbing, for your salvation depends on it. There are some who think they are playing it safe by having one foot on one mountain and another foot on the other mountain. They hope a mixture of their good works and God's good works will be what it takes. But by doing so they belittle and despise the life and death of Christ and His righteousness He has given us and inflate their own self righteousness to compensate for what Christ supposedly couldn't do. God did not die for only the sins you couldn't atone for yourself. He died for all your sins. Now is the time to confess your sins and allow God to save you. Let Him impart His righteousness to you, to make you spiritually clean and fill you with His Holy Spirit and place you at the foot of Mt. Zion.

If you are uncertain of your salvation or are faced with the reality you have been trying to climb both mountains, take the time to repent, to turn from your sin, to confess your total dependence on God for your salvation, and pray the following prayer in faith:

Dear Heavenly Father,

I am sorry for rejecting You and living my life to please me. I am sorry for my disobedience and doing wrong when I knew it was wrong. I confess that there is no good work that I could produce that would measure up to Your standard of holiness. Any good within me or any good I could do comes up short to Your glory and Your standard. Forgive me for trying to earn my salvation and to do what You have already done for me. My confidence and faith is now placed in Your Son, Jesus Christ, Who died on the cross for my sins. It is Your blood that cleanses me from all unrighteousness, makes me into a brand new creation and makes me holy and able to stand in Your presence. I give my heart and life to You, Jesus, and give You permission to guide and direct me the rest of my life.

Amen.

If you prayed the above prayer of salvation, welcome to the family of God! Your salvation is secured in Jesus and not on what you do or don't do. Rest in that reality! Now as a response to your new relationship in Christ, begin to live for Him and pursue Him that you may grow in revelation and wisdom of your Savior. It is also important that you tell someone about your decision, even if it was a rededication. The Bible says to repent and be baptized in water. That's your next mission! Go and tell your pastor you wish to be baptized. If you don't have a church, go find a healthy, Bible-believing, people-loving, God-loving church in your area. God gives us family, our brothers and sisters in the Lord, to help one another grow in Christ and to fulfill His purpose.

If you would like additional prayer or advice on how to pick a church family please refer to the contact information at the back of this book. I would love to help. If you made a decision or rededicated your life I also want to hear from you. I want to rejoice with you!

The King of the Mountain is Waiting

Our God is a self-disclosing God who desires to reveal Himself to His creation. God is calling you unto Himself. He is asking you to leave the valley of day to day existence and the life as usual mindset and invites you to ascend His holy mountain. He has paid a great price and is eager for you to accept the invitation and begin the ascent.

I invite you to come along and climb with Moses beginning in the valley at the foot of Mt. Sinai. As you journey up the mountain, I pray

God to supernaturally prepare you for the ascent, to sanctify and renew your mind and heart, that He will illuminate your imagination, and that at every step, every station along the mountain He will promote you to experience greater levels of revelation and knowledge of His Glory.

To climb the mountain of Zion is to pursue His presence; there is no other way to fellowship with the Father. Moses ascended an earthly Mt. Sinai, the believer ascends a spiritual Mt. Zion. The natural path, process and progression of Moses' journey up Mt. Sinai and into the presence of God as recorded in Exodus twenty-four mirrors the spiritual path every believer must make to pursue God and fellowship with Him.

Are you ready to climb? The King of the mountain is calling you to Come Up! To fellowship with The King of the Mountain, to experience greater measures of His presence and power, you must first draw nigh and ascend.

Which Mountain Are You Climbing?

Mt. Sinai	**Mt. Zion**
Natural	Supernatural
Old Covenant	New Covenant
Moses	Jesus
Law	Gospel
Salvation by Works	Salvation by Grace
Focus on Man	Focus on God
Focus is Doing	Focus is Being
The Law Condemns	The Gospel Justifies
Separation	Reconciliation
Breeds Fear	Breeds Faith
Magnifies man's weakness	Magnifies God's power

Come Up!

Then He said to Moses, "Come up to the LORD, you and Aaron, Nadab and Abihu and seventy of the elders of Israel, and you shall worship at a distance.

Exodus 24:1

Moses went up to God, and the LORD called to him from the mountain...

Exodus 19:3

The LORD came down on Mount Sinai, to the top of the mountain; and the LORD called Moses to the top of the mountain, and Moses went up.

Exodus 19:20

And He said, "Come!" And Peter got out of the boat, and walked on the water and came toward Jesus.

Matthew 14:29

I press on toward the goal for the prize of the upward call of God in Christ Jesus.

Philippians 3:14

The Spirit and the bride say, "Come." And let the one who hears say, "Come." And let the one who is thirsty come; let the one who wishes take the water of life without cost.

Revelation 22:17

See to it that you do not refuse Him who is speaking...

Hebrews 12:25

1

Invitation

X Marks the Spot

I was at a big shopping mall for the first time and needed to find a department store. I walked through the main entrance and up to a large mall directory sign. After scanning the list of stores I finally located the store I needed. "Great!" I thought, "This should be easy." But I still stood there for several minutes, perplexed and without a clue which way to go. I could see my store, the full layout of the mall, and still wasn't sure how to get there. You know what was missing? There was no big arrow or X on that mall directory that pointed to where I was standing. Even though I had a detailed and accurate map in front of me, I was still lost. To get where I needed to go, I first had to know where I was. A successful trek into the presence of God requires you to know where you're starting from. Let's get started.

At the Foot of the Mountain

> *Then He said to Moses, "Come up to the LORD, you and Aaron, Nadab and Abihu and seventy of the elders of Israel,*
> *Exodus 24:1*

God could have come all the way down to where the people of Israel were encamped, but He didn't. He called Moses and the elders out of the valley and up to the mountain top. Rather than meet them in the valley, He descended only so far, as low as the highest mountain peak in their sight, and commanded them to leave their habitation. God pursues us when we are lost and dead in sin. Now that we have been found, our response must be to pursue God. God responded differently to the Israelites when they were held captive by the Egyptians. (Ex. 2:23-25; 3:7-10) They were enslaved and unable to respond to a call to the mountain even if it had been given. So He sent them a savior, Moses, a type of Christ, who delivered them from their oppressors with mighty manifestations of His miraculous power.

Access to the Mountain Has Been Granted

God delivered the Israelites from Egypt so they could meet Him at the mountain to worship. He did for them what they couldn't do for themselves. He has done the same for you. All mankind is born into spiritual slavery, which is sin. We are bound, trapped and unable to free ourselves from its control. Sin is like a spiritual disease that leads to death and starts by attacking and destroying our spiritual senses. Our physical senses of sight, hearing, touch, taste and smell make it possible for us to know and interact with the natural world around us. The physical senses are the gateways to physical realities. Spiritual senses do in the spiritual world what physical senses do in the natural world; they enable us to connect, interact, know and experience the spiritual world. Ultimately, they provide a way to know and experience God. (Jn. 4:24) Sin, like a disease, distorts, severs, and destroys our ability to know and relate to God. Jesus, the Great Physician, is our hope and His blood is the antidote. The Bible tells us, *"Without the shedding of blood there can be no forgiveness of sins.".* (Heb. 9:22)

In the Old Testament, before Jesus came to earth, God would accept the life, or the blood of an animal, offered to Him as a substitute payment on behalf of the sins of the offender. In our helpless state we are unable to respond to an invitation to the presence of God. In our lostness God sent a Savior, His Son Jesus Christ, to set us free from our captor, the devil, to heal us from our sin sickness. We have been delivered from the slavery of sin so that we may have the freedom to journey up the mountain and worship God our redeemer and rescuer. At the moment of our salvation He destroyed the work of the devil, He removed our filthy rags, He set us free from the law of sin and death and finally, once and for all, made it possible for us to know, experience, and love Him. No other way was possible. At the moment of your salvation, He placed you supernaturally at the foot of Mt. Zion, and beckoned you to pursue Him in fellowship. The author of Hebrews makes the connection between a physical mountain, Mt. Sinai, and a spiritual mountain, Mt. Zion, for us in Hebrews twelve:

> *For you have not come to a mountain that can be touched and to a blazing fire, and to darkness and gloom and whirlwind,...But you have come to Mount Zion...*
>
> *Hebrews 12:18,22*

A beautiful and magnificent parallel from the natural to the spiritual for believers today is the example of the Hebrews being set free from Egyptian slavery by Moses and led out to worship God at Mt. Sinai. You were set free from your slavery to sin and led by Christ to the foot of the spiritual Mt. Zion. God set you free and placed you at the foot of the mountain so you may pursue Him!

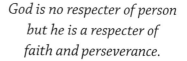

God is no respecter of person but he is a respecter of faith and perseverance.

Mt. Zion, His Holy Hill, represents the manifest and abiding presence of God. Climbing Mt. Zion is pressing in and pursuing the presence and person of Jesus. When God calls you to Himself, He cries out from the mountain peak, "Come up!" just as He called Moses.

The Call is an Upward Call in Christ Jesus

At the moment of you salvation in Christ, the Bible Says God supernaturally raised you up and placed you with Him in the heavenly places in Christ Jesus:

> and raised us up with Him, and seated us with Him in the heavenly places in Christ Jesus, so that in the ages to come He might show the surpassing riches of His grace in kindness toward us in Christ Jesus.
>
> Ephesians 2:6-7

When God saved you from you sins, He supernaturally placed you in Him on the mountain. Your identity and position is no longer as a sinner bound and tormented by Satan but as a saint, freed from sin and seated with Christ. God didn't just rescue you from sin, He transported you in the spirit to sit next to Christ. The call of God is an upward call in Christ Jesus. The Apostle Paul understood this when he said:

> I press on toward the goal for the prize of the upward call of God in Christ Jesus.
>
> Philippians 3:14

You now have the supernatural capacity to connect and commune with God any time or any place. No matter where you go in the natural, in the supernatural, you have been seated with Christ. When you are tempted, tested and tried to sin, remind your flesh of your new position in Christ. You have been called and seated with Christ!

The Call is a Call to Maturity

The upward call is also a call to maturity. God has given apostles, prophets, evangelists, pastors and teachers for building up the body of Christ to maturity:

for the equipping of the saints for the work of service, to the building up of the body of Christ; until we all attain to the unity of the faith, and of the knowledge of the Son of God, to a mature man, to the measure of the stature which belongs to the fullness of Christ.

Ephesians 4:12,13

Apostles, prophets, evangelists, pastors and teachers are like mountain guides God has given us to show us the way up Mt. Zion. Do not neglect or underestimate the power and influence these gifts, and the people that walk in them, have to guide you up the mountain of God. Pray and seek out those who operate in the apostolic, or prophetic, or evangelistic, pastoral or teaching gifts and spend time with them. When you connect yourself with these God-appointed gifts to the Body of Christ they will fast-forward you up the mountain and accelerate your spiritual growth in Christ.

You Are as Close to God as You Choose to Be

In the letter of James he was writing to believers when he said, "Draw nigh to God and He will draw nigh to you." (James 4:8) Who does the moving first? You do. There is no one to blame for your lack of intimacy and fellowship with God. You are as close to God as you choose to be. God in calling you into greater depths of relationship and closeness to Him, but you must take the first step. You are at the base of the mountain and experiencing God as well as a person can from a distance. Greater and deeper manifestations of God's power, love, peace and presence in your life are only possible further up the mountain. You have to move first, and then He moves toward you. Why is it this way? Read carefully as I share with you a powerful principle: God gives us what we need, but we must pursue the deeper things of God. God is no respecter of person but he is a respecter of faith and perseverance. The woman with the issue of blood in Luke chapter eight received her answer to prayer, the healing of her body,

15

because she pressed in through the crowd, believing if she could only touch the hem of His robe, she would be made whole again. Many were clamoring, pushing and touching Jesus, but it was her touch that caused Jesus to stop in His tracks. It was her persistence and tenacity, fueled by her faith in the power of Jesus, that led to her miracle. She was not going to be denied her healing even if it meant crawling on all fours through the crowd. Are you one who is content to watch Jesus from a safe distance? Where has that gotten you? Some people wonder why they have so little of God when God has so little of them.

> *Some people wonder why they have so little of God when God has so little of them.*

He did for you what you could not do for yourself. Now it's time for you to respond to His voice in faith and courage, and leaving the comforts of the valley behind, begin the journey for which you were created and equipped.

In the Old Testament you had to have a personal invitation from God to experience His presence. It was a privilege for the select few. Now in the New Testament that invitation extends beyond prophets, kings and priests to include all who call out to the Lord!

Valley Campers and Mountain Climbers

In the shadow of the mountain the Israelites camped to await the next direction from Moses:

> *When they set out from Rephidim, they came to the wilderness of Sinai and camped in the wilderness; and there Israel camped in front of the mountain.*
>
> *Exodus 19:2*

It was there that God descended and enveloped the mountain in a mighty storm of thunder, lightning, trumpet blasts and smoke:

All the people perceived the thunder and the lightning flashes and the sound of the trumpet and the mountain smoking; and when the people saw it, they trembled and stood at a distance. Then they said to Moses, "Speak to us yourself and we will listen; but let not God speak to us, or we will die."

Exodus 20:18-19

This awesome and terrible demonstration of God struck terror and fear in the hearts of everyone, including Moses. This manifestation of God was no accident. Even though they were terrified, Moses encouraged them to not be afraid for this was a test. God was instilling His fear in them so they would resist the temptation to disobey and sin against God:

Moses said to the people, "Do not be afraid; for God has come in order to test you, and in order that the fear of Him may remain with you, so that you may not sin.

Exodus 20:20

But the children of Israel did not listen to Moses and instead *"they trembled and stood at a distance."* They decided the risk was too great and concluded it would be safer for them to let Moses take the risk of experiencing the awesome and terrifying presence of God, and then allow him to relay his encounters and words from God to them after he had descended, if he returned from the mountain at all! They had chosen to have a second-hand relationship with God, to know and follow Him from a distance through a mediator, rather than encounter Him for themselves. Many believers do this today. Rather than ascend the mountain and pursue Christ and His presence they wait until Sunday or perhaps a midweek Bible study to hear the message from the Lord delivered by their pastor, or their "Moses", and they are content with the weekly second-hand, hand-me-down transaction. I thank God for the pastors who have poured into my life through sermons. I need those "Moses's" in my life, but if the only time I get a Word from the Lord is if it's through the mouth of another I'm a valley camper and no different than the Israelites who choose to stay in the camp rather than risk an encounter with the God of the mountain.

Fear of God will keep you close to the mountain. The love of God will drive you to the top. A fear mentality is a slave mentality. Fear keeps you on the right path as long as you know the boss is watching. You need the fear of God..."*the fear of the Lord is the BEGINNING of knowledge*". (*Prov. 1:7*). It's where it starts. In the valley at the foot of the mountain is close but not enough. But sadly it is where many choose to remain--living the Christian life because you have to, not doing because of the consequences. The children of Israel feared God, so much so they were content to have Moses be their mediator-the go between. They were content to watch the activities of God from a distance, from the valley, and wait on Moses to deliver the message.

> *Fear of God will keep you close to the mountain. The love of God will drive you to the top.*

So are you a camper or a climber? Are you going to remain at the foot of the mountain and be content living vicariously through the God-encounters and revelations of others or are you going to accept the invitation of God and answer the upward call to leave the valley behind and climb the mountain of God? I hope you've become dissatisfied with camping and are ready to put on some spiritual hiking boots because now it's time leave the valley behind and Come Worship!

Come Worship!

Then He said to Moses, "Come up to the LORD, you and Aaron, Nadab and Abihu and seventy of the elders of Israel, and you shall worship at a distance.

Exodus 24:1

Exalt the LORD our God And worship at His holy hill, For holy is the LORD our God.

Psalm 99:9

Let us go into His dwelling place; Let us worship at His footstool.

Psalm 132:7

2

Adoration

And You Shall Worship

The main purpose of God's invitation to Moses and his followers to come up on the mountain was so they could worship God. *"Come up to the Lord...and you shall worship..."* (Ex. 24:1) He made His expectation very clear from the beginning when He first appeared to Moses in the burning bush that He was delivering them from Egypt to *"worship God at this mountain"*. (Ex. 3:12) God's purpose for you is the same. Just as He delivered the Hebrews from the bondage of Egypt and led them to the mountain that they might worship Him, so He has saved you and led you to a spiritual mountain. And upon that mountain, Mt. Zion, in the presence of your Creator, you have been called to worship!

To understand more fully this calling we must first understand what worship means; and more specifically, what kind of worship does God expect of us?

According to the World English Dictionary, the word "worship" means "to show profound religious devotion and respect to; adore or venerate". It is composed of the root word "worth" and the suffix "-ship". Worth means to give honor, reverence, respect, high regard or value and the suffix "-ship" indicates rank, office or position. Merging these two definitions together, at its base and fundamental level, to worship is to give someone or something a high regard and place of value and position.

God Wants Your All and Your Awe

To worship God means to give God your very best and to love Him with all your heart and it has a two-fold expression: One is your complete obedience even at the expense of great personal sacrifice,

> God wants your all and your awe. He wants all your obedience and all your adoration.

and the other is to possess a feeling of respect, awe and reverence. God wants your all and your awe. He wants all your obedience and all your adoration. To give Him your all in worship means that each and every day, *"you present your body a living and holy sacrifice"* (Rom. 12:1) –to worship Him with your life through your words, thoughts and actions. To give Christ your all in worship means to grow in the awareness of His presence and live each moment in Christ, for Christ, through Christ and because of Christ. To give Him your awe means your worship comes from the heart, the seat of your emotions, and it is sincere, or truthful. This type of worship is illustrated well in Revelation 4 (I suggest you go read the whole chapter right now) when the Apostle John was taken to Heaven. He describes a spectacular scene around the Throne of God where there are twenty four elders and four "living creatures". In response to the awesomeness and glory of God the "living creatures" cry out day and night and never stop declaring:

> *HOLY, HOLY, HOLY is THE LORD GOD, THE ALMIGHTY, WHO WAS AND WHO IS AND WHO IS TO COME.*
>
> Revelation 4:8

The heavenly hosts are in awe of God continually as He manifests

His glory to them in greater and greater measures. There is no end to His holiness, His awesomeness, and every time they declare, *"Holy, holy, holy"* it is not from repetition or habit but is a genuine response to a greater revelation of His holiness. Having been touched by the glory of God, they respond in awe.

Worship & Sacrifice

Let's continue our study of worship. Closely associated to worship is sacrifice. In order to understand worship we must include sacrifice.

The first time the word worship is mentioned in the Bible is in Genesis 22. Here God asks Abraham to sacrifice his son Isaac on Mt. Moriah:

> *He said, "Take now your son, your only son, whom you love, Isaac, and go to the land of Moriah, and offer him there as a burnt offering on one of the mountains of which I will tell you."*
>
> *Genesis 22:2*

Abraham travels three days with Isaac and finally arrives at the appointed destination. Notice what Abraham says to his servants [young men] next:

> *Abraham said to his young men, "Stay here with the donkey, and I and the lad will go over there; and we will worship and return to you."*
>
> *Genesis 22:5*

He does not say "we will sacrifice" but "we will worship" and return. Abraham understood the connection between worship and sacrifice. To worship God, to give him allegiance in your life will require sacrifice. Just as God tested Abraham's allegiance and devotion or worship to God, God will test you as well.

Later in Exodus we see a similar connection when God is calling Moses to deliver the Hebrews from the Egyptians:

> And He said, "Certainly I will be with you, and this shall be the sign to you that it is I who have sent you: when you have brought the people out of Egypt, you shall worship God at this mountain."
>
> Exodus 3:12

God tells Moses He will be with him, and to confirm it He declares they will worship God at Mt. Sinai. Then just six verses later God again is telling Moses what to say and what is going to happen. Notice what message God tells Moses to deliver to Pharaoh:

> They will pay heed to what you say; and you with the elders of Israel will come to the king of Egypt and you will say to him, 'The LORD, the God of the Hebrews, has met with us. So now, please, let us go a three days' journey into the wilderness, that we may sacrifice to the LORD our God.'
>
> Exodus 3:18

Here the phrase, "that we may sacrifice to the LORD our God." is used. There is an intimate connection between worship and sacrifice.

The Apostle Paul brings more clarification to the meaning of worship and its connection to sacrifice in his letter to the church in Rome:

> Therefore I urge you, brethren, by the mercies of God, to present your bodies a living and holy sacrifice, acceptable to God, which is your spiritual service of worship.
>
> Romans 12:1

The Apostle Paul is very clear that presenting your body as a living sacrifice is your spiritual service of worship. It is part of giving God your all. In other words, living a life of dedication and obedience to God, which will demand sacrifice, is in and of itself an act of worship unto God.

In your journey up the mountain of God you will spend your entire life learning how to give God your all and awe. As you grow in intimacy and relationship and obedience with God He will reveal greater measures of His glory that will overwhelm you, and in awe you will cry out as the "living creatures" do in Revelation four, *"Holy, holy, holy is the Lord God, the Almighty!"*

What Does Worship Look Like?

In a broad sense, anything you do with the attitude and purpose of glorifying God is an act of worship. So, if when you are washing the dishes after a meal you are praising God and doing it in excellence and with a grateful heart, you are offering up worship. With this in mind practically anything you do can be used to glorify and worship God. And you should keep in mind and practice the active awareness and purpose of worshiping God in everything you do.

On a more specific level, the following are seven expressions of worship to express your all and awe of God.

7 Expressions of Worship to Express Your All and Awe of God

1.   *Worship God with a Thankful Heart*

> *Bless the LORD, O my soul, And forget none of His benefits; Who pardons all your iniquities, Who heals all your diseases; Who redeems your life from the pit, Who crowns you with loving kindness and compassion; Who satisfies your years with good things, So that your youth is renewed like the eagle.*
>
> *Psalm 103:2-5*

Ascending the Mountain of God

God gives us so many good reasons to worship Him. One of the easiest ways to worship God is to specifically thank Him for all of your many blessings. Make a list and write down as many reasons you can think of to be thankful. Start with blessings that benefit you personally. For example, perhaps your job, your good health, a home, food in the refrigerator, your children, your grandchildren, etc. Then include spiritual blessings such as thanking God for your salvation, the fruit of the Spirit, and the abilities and talents He has given you. Thank Him for loving you, protecting you, and guiding you. You can see how these are slightly different from blessings that benefit you personally-they focus more on the spiritual than the natural.

But there is yet one more level of thankfulness, that when practiced, will revolutionize your worship: Reverse the focus from yourself and center the focus of thankfulness on who and what God is. Thank God for His many qualities and characteristics such as His love, His holiness, His faithfulness, His patience, His all powerfulness, and His all knowingness—these are just a few to get you going. When you shift into this third level of thankfulness, it removes the self-centered thankfulness,not bad in and of itself—we are thankful for the goodness of God towards us too—we just have to begin somewhere. Shifting our thankfulness focus off of ourselves and more towards God elevates it to a more pure expression of worship that is truly God-centered. It is important to practice being thankful often in your worship of God. We regularly fill our mind with negative and selfish thoughts, and actively thinking of your blessings will improve your attitude and outlook on life.

> *Shifting our thankfulness focus off of ourselves and more towards God elevates it to a more pure expression of worship that is truly God-centered.*

2.   *Worship God by Giving Him Your Best*

One popular and important expression of worship is the Praise and Worship service in the local church. This is called corporate worship and involves a group of people singing and worshiping God together. This is a wonderful experience and should be practiced often. Sometimes churches will have a worship emphasis and focus the service on worship rather than on preaching. Participate fully and actively in these worship settings. Forget about the cares and stresses of life and center your thoughts and feelings on giving God all the glory due His Name. Some people tend to be reserve while others let it all hang out. Don't let someone else's worship of God distract you, and also don't be shy to express your love and devotion to God. He is a wonderful God and deserves the highest praise!

> *Bless the LORD, O my soul, And all that is within me, bless His holy name.*
>
> *Psalm 103:1*

3.   *Worship God in Spirit and in Truth*

As a child growing up in a small charismatic church during the late 70's and early 80's we sang our fair share of choruses. I fondly remember singing songs like *"He Has Made Me Glad"*, *"As the Deer"*, *"This is the Day"*, *"Jehovah Jireh"*, *"Don't You Know it's Time to Praise the Lord"*, *"Give Me Oil in My Lamp"*, just to mention a few. I loved working the overhead and putting the transparencies with lyrics on the projector to be shown on the wall. Just thinking about these songs prepares my spirit to enter into worship. If you're over forty years old and grew up in a Charismatic or Pentecostal church, I just sent you down memory lane. Go ahead, put this book down and get your praise on! You can come back down off the mountain later and continue where you left off.

As a young teenager in the late 80's and early 90's my family joined the local Assembly of God church in town and there I was introduced to the hymn book. I was a budding trumpet player and would play on the worship team every Sunday and Wednesday night. It was there I cut my teeth on hymns like, *"At the Cross", "Oh, How I love Jesus", "He Lives", "When We All Get to Heaven", "When the Roll Is Called up Yonder"* and my favorite because I thought I could play some cool licks was, *"I'll Fly Away"*.

At some point from the 90's and on through the 2,000's we entered the contemporary Christian music era. During this transition for me I laid down the hymn book and now with technological advances went to watching the lyrics from a video projector on a big video screen. Stand up pianos were replaced with keyboards and amazing graphics were incorporated to enhance the worship experience. I loved singing songs like *"Open the Eyes of My Heart", "I Am Free", "How Great is Our God", ""Here I am to Worship"*, and *"Days of Elijah,"* just to mention a few.

And now as time marches on, the mid 2000's and the corporate worship experience continues to develop and evolve within the culture and technology. I love the heart and nuances of every era of worship I've grown up in and do not believe one is any better than another. Yet I have seen churches split over the issue of whether to offer a traditional or contemporary worship service. Sadly they have mistaken the mold for the gold. God does not prefer one kind of style of music over another. What He prefers is for His children to worship Him in spirit and in truth:

> *But an hour is coming, and now is, when the true worshipers will worship the Father in spirit and truth; for such people the Father seeks to be His worshipers. "God is spirit, and those who worship Him must worship in spirit and truth.*
> *John 4:23-24*

We all have our favorite praise and worship songs, and to think of them fast-forwards us into the presence of God. When you come across a worship song you particularly like, take the time and effort to get the lyrics. Download the song on your mp3 player and check out the other music from the author too. Build your own praise and worship song list that should continually grow. For most of my favorite songs I print out the lyrics and put them in a binder that I use for prayer and devotions. Build your own worship lyrics binder and it will become a precious tool for you to enhance your mountain top experiences.

4.   *Worship God with a Joyful Noise*

> *Give thanks to the LORD with the lyre; Sing praises to Him with a harp of ten strings.*
>
> *Psalms 33:2*

As an adult I learned to play the guitar so I could enhance my worship experience. I'm still not that good but it doesn't matter. Whenever I hear a song I like, I can generally find a simple chord chart and there's always a YouTube video for beginners to find to see and hear it played. There are times I'll spend the majority of my worship time learning and practicing a new worship song on my guitar. These times have greatly increased and enhanced my times with God.

You don't have to play an instrument to make a joyful noise unto the Lord. We have all been commanded to sing and worship our Creator. Here are just a few scriptures:

> *Sing praises to God, sing praises; Sing praises to our King, sing praises.*
>
> *Psalms 47:6*

> *Sing praises to the LORD, who dwells in Zion; Declare among the peoples His deeds.*
>
> *Psalms 9:11*

> *My heart is steadfast, O God, my heart is steadfast; I will sing, yes, I will sing praises!*
>
> *Psalms 57:7*

Sing to the LORD a new song; Sing to the LORD, all the earth.

Psalms 96:1

Shout joyfully to the LORD, all the earth; Break forth and sing for joy and sing praises.

Psalms 98:4

Praise the LORD! Sing to the LORD a new song, And His praise in the congregation of the godly ones.

Psalms 149:1

God has gifted some with amazing voices and they can use their voices to sing in the choir or sing solos that bring glory to God, but for the rest of us we will make a joyful noise unto the Lord in other ways. Singing praise and worship songs during your alone time with God will bless and bring glory to His Name. He created your voice, and your musical ability, or the lack thereof, but when you sing from the heart and sing in spirit and in truth, you please God because that is what He wants from you:

O clap your hands, all peoples; Shout to God with the voice of joy.

Psalms 47:1

Raise a song, strike the timbrel, The sweet sounding lyre with the harp.

Psalms 81:2

Praise Him with trumpet sound; Praise Him with harp and lyre. Praise Him with timbrel and dancing; Praise Him with stringed instruments and pipe. Praise Him with loud cymbals; Praise Him with resounding cymbals.

Psalms 150:3-5

5.   *Worship with Your Hands and Feet*

Let them praise His name with dancing...

Psalms 149:3

Imagine you just were told you had won a million dollars. How would you react? You'd likely be shouting, jumping, clapping, spinning, and throwing your hands in the air. You couldn't keep still with so much emotion coursing through your body. You've been given something far more valuable and eternal than a winning lottery ticket. You've been given the priceless gift of salvation and have been saved from your sins! You now have the hope of spending an eternity with God in Heaven. Let that reality get a hold of you and you won't stay still for long—it makes no difference if you're an introvert or extrovert, conservative or expressive. That kind of joy consumes the whole body. Don't let pride rob you of worshiping God with your whole body.

6.   *Worship God in Your Giving.*

After coming into the house they saw the Child with Mary
His mother; and they fell to the ground and worshiped Him.
Then, opening their treasures, they presented to Him gifts
of gold, frankincense, and myrrh.

Matthew 2:11

Giving is a genuine and appropriate act of devotion and worship to God. The wise men expressed their worship to the baby Jesus through the giving of precious and expensive gifts. True and sincere love is marked by giving of oneself. The Gospel of John declares, *"For God so loved the world that he gave..."*

Some of the most pure and powerful expressions of worship we can offer God is through our creative gifts and abilities.

(John 3:16) In our desire to please God through our worship we should naturally desire to give Him the best of our time, talent and treasure:

And do not neglect doing good and sharing, for with such sacrifices God is pleased.

Hebrews 13:16

The author of Hebrews gives us two examples of worship that bring pleasure to God: doing good and sharing. Remember that worship and sacrifice are intimately connected. In our worship to God we should regularly look for and include acts of kindness and generosity in our day to day life. Feeding the homeless, helping a struggling mother by taking her kids school clothes shopping, dropping off a homemade meal for a neighbor in need, and giving away clothes in your closet to a person you know could use them, all are examples of doing good and sharing and are each expressions of worship to God. Any time you use your specific gifts and resources to meet the needs of others, your good deeds and generosity become sacrifices of praise and worship and are pleasing to God.

But I have received everything in full and have an abundance; I am amply supplied, having received from Epaphroditus what you have sent, a fragrant aroma, an acceptable sacrifice, well-pleasing to God.

Philippians 4:18

7.   *Worship God Through Your Creativity*

Five times in Psalms we are told to sing to the Lord a new song (Ps. 33:3; 96:1;144:9; 149:1) Psalms 40:3 says: *"He put a new song in my mouth, a song of praise to our God..."* The prophet Isaiah declared:

Sing to the LORD a new song, Sing His praise from the end of the earth!

Isaiah 42:10

Our God is a creative God—just look at the complexity and diversity of the creation and the universe around us, and He has deposited His creative spark within you.

Some of the most pure and powerful expressions of worship we can offer God is through our creative gifts and abilities. Worship Him by creating a poem, a song, or a play. Are you good with art? Then use your favorite medium—pencil, pen, oil, water colors, canvas or computer—and let the Holy Spirit inspire you! Prefer more tangible art? Then worship God through pottery, or sewing, or crochet, or beading, or any of the other countless ways to create works of art that bring glory to God. And just as the quality of our voice does not matter to God when we sing and make a joyful noise unto the Lord, neither does our artistic abilities, or the lack thereof, of any importance to God. What matters is that you offer up a new song, a new painting, a new patchwork quilt, a new piece of pottery or handmade jewelry, a new poem or play or story to Him, and by giving it our very best they become priceless treasures we lay at the feet of Jesus, just as the wise men did as they worshipped their newborn King.

God has created and called you to worship Him. He calls to you from His holy mountain to worship His holy name. Present your body as a living sacrifice and worship God with all that is within you. Worship Him with a new song. Worship Him with your time, talents and treasures. Worship Him in your good deeds and generosity. Worship Him with your creative abilities. Above all, worship Him in spirit and in truth, for those are the worshippers our God seeks. Worship prepares the heart for the next step up the mountain, the call to consecration, the call to Come Out!

Praise the LORD! Praise God in His sanctuary; Praise Him in His mighty expanse.

Praise Him for His mighty deeds; Praise Him according to His excellent greatness.

Praise Him with trumpet sound; Praise Him with harp and lyre.

Praise Him with timbrel and dancing; Praise Him with stringed instruments and pipe.

Praise Him with loud cymbals; Praise Him with resounding cymbals.

Let everything that has breath praise the LORD. Praise the LORD!

Psalms 150:1-6

Come Out!

*Moses then wrote down everything the LORD had said.
He got up early the next morning and built an altar at
the foot of the mountain and set up twelve stone pillars
representing the twelve tribes of Israel. Then he sent young
men of the children of Israel, who offered burnt offerings
and sacrificed peace offerings of oxen to the LORD.*

Exodus 24:4-5

*The LORD also said to Moses, "Go to the people and
consecrate them today and tomorrow, and let them wash
their garments; and let them be ready for the third day, for
on the third day the LORD will come down on Mount Sinai
in the sight of all the people.*

Exodus 19:10-11

*And Moses brought the people out of the camp to meet God,
and they stood at the foot of the mountain.*

Exodus 19:17

3

Consecration

There are many obstacles that inhibit mountaineers from success: falling rocks or ice, avalanches, ice and snow slopes, crevasses, inclement weather, and altitude, among many other deterrents. But often it's excess weight that can be the biggest obstacle. Experienced climbers know the value of eliminating any extra weights and carrying only what is absolutely essential for the expedition. Non-essentials are excess weight and suck up vital energy resources. The extra weight seems insignificant at first, but when weariness and fatigue set in, dropping those little extras can often be the difference between failure and success.

Just because Mt. Zion is a spiritual mountain does not mean it doesn't have its own set of obstacles and challenges. In this chapter we will explore some of the obstacles spiritual mountaineers must contend with as they prepare for the climb up the mountain.

The Altar of Sacrifice

Early in the morning before Moses began the ascent up the mountain he built an altar at the foot of the mountain and set up twelve pillars of rocks to represent the twelve tribes of Israel. It was upon this altar he sacrificed burnt offerings and fellowship offerings unto the Lord on behalf of the people:

Moses then wrote down everything the LORD had said.
He got up early the next morning and built an altar at
the foot of the mountain and set up twelve stone pillars
representing the twelve tribes of Israel. Then he sent young
men of the children of Israel, who offered burnt offerings
and sacrificed peace offerings of oxen to the LORD.

Exodus 24:4-5

It is significant sacrifices were offered first, before the ascent. Before you enter the Presence of God it is vital to seek forgiveness, the purpose of the Burnt Offering, and offer thanksgiving, the purpose of the Fellowship Offering.

The Burnt Offerings were voluntary acts of worship to atone, or appease the judgment of God, for unintentional sins. The burnt offerings were a willful and proactive expression of devotion, commitment and complete surrender to God. You should always approach God first with a repentant heart seeking His forgiveness and His righteousness to atone for your sins. No one can ascend the mountain on their won strength, or own terms. It is by His grace we have been placed at the mountain, it is His grace that allows us to press in and press up. Disobedience and sin in our lives acts like extra weights that keep us from reaching our potential in Christ. The spiritual mountaineer does well to regularly and often invite the light of the Holy Spirit to search his or her heart and expose any unforgiveness or unconfessed sins.

The Fellowship Offerings were also voluntary acts of worship; to offer thanksgiving for the goodness of God and the gift of being in relationship with Him. Once the heart has been cleansed a natural and right response is thanksgiving and praise to God. A thankful heart often begins with a self-centered focus. We thank Him for our health, our things, the

Mature thanksgiving gives God the glory for who He is, more so than what He has done for me.

blessings of God that improve our life, but mature thanksgiving leaves the self and travels upward and focuses upon the general and specific attributes of God, becoming less self-centered and more God-centered. Mature thanksgiving gives God the glory for who He is, more so than what He has done for me. Focusing on God's love, power, holiness, are appropriate and needed expressions of worship and thanksgiving to God.

The next time you are worshipping God notice what you are thanking Him for. Are your expressions of gratitude more you-focused or God-focused? Remember, both are appropriate and needed but make a point to shift your gratitude to who God is rather than just on what He has done for you. If this is new territory for you then you may need to do a Bible study on the qualities and characteristics of God. The following are some Scriptures that highlight various characteristics of God. Take some time to meditate on them and allow them to shift your thankfulness on God:

Scriptures to Shift Your Thankfulness on God

Oh, the depth of the riches both of the wisdom and knowledge of God! How unsearchable are His judgments and unfathomable His ways!

Romans 11:33

"Listen to this, O Job, Stand and consider the wonders of God. "Do you know how God establishes them, And makes the lightning of His cloud to shine?

Job 37:14-15

"Is anything too difficult for the LORD? At the appointed time I will return to you, at this time next year, and Sarah will have a son."

Genesis 18:14

The eyes of the LORD are in every place, Watching the evil and the good.

Proverbs 15:3

"Am I a God who is near," declares the LORD, "And not a God far off? "Can a man hide himself in hiding places So I do not see him?" declares the LORD. "Do I not fill the heavens and the earth?" declares the LORD.

Jeremiah 23:23-24

Before the mountains were born Or You gave birth to the earth and the world, Even from everlasting to everlasting, You are God.

Psalms 90:2

In Salvation God Chooses You. In Consecration You Choose God.

Now that we have laid a foundation for repentance and thankfulness let's explore more fully the next step up the mountain, the act of consecration.

Consecration is willingly and knowingly laying your life on the altar of sacrifice, it is your response to such a wonderful salvation, it is the response asked of God, expected of God, required of God for those who are Presence driven. In salvation our decision is based out of necessity. God saves us from ourselves, our mess, our lostness, and our sin. He cleanses us on the inside, sets us free from the death penalty of sin and places a robe of righteousness upon our shoulders. He then declares us innocent, justified before God through His Son Jesus Christ. Now He cries "Come up!" and there we stand, between us and the foot of the mountain is an altar. We have been put in right standing with God

Consecration that starts you up the path into His presence responds to John 3:16 by crying out, "For I so love God that I give my only life to Him."

but we were not called to stand-still, but to move up, to climb. The first ledge, the first peak, the mountain climber for God is to climb onto is the altar of sacrifice, and upon this altar lay down our life willingly, graciously, obediently. It is upon this altar we declare our allegiance and dedication to God.

The consecrated life is a life of separation, a defining moment where we decidedly move towards God. In salvation He declares His love to us. In consecration we declare our love to Him. In salvation God chooses us. In consecration we choose God. In salvation God does the work-we are passive recipients of His grace. But in consecration we begin the work, we respond to His invitation and He empowers us to do something we'd never been able to do before, move towards God inspired and empowered by His grace. Before Christ, our attempts to be good or reach out to God were rooted in self righteous works. We were really, to be honest, consecrating ourselves, or making ourselves holy for God, that is the mountain of Sinai. But on Mt. Zion, in response to His love and grace, He empowers us and we give over our life through the act of consecration and He makes us Holy—it is a beautiful transaction—our filthy rags of unrighteousness in exchange for His mantle of grace.

John 3:16 demonstrates the depth and magnitude of God's love to us in salvation: *"For God so loved the world that He gave his only Son."* Our response to the gift of His Son also demonstrates our love for Him. Consecration that starts you up the path into His presence responds to John 3:16 by crying out, "For I so love God that I give my only life to Him."

The following are ten significant areas of life that can be obstacles or weights that keep us from the presence of God if not anticipated and surrendered to the Lordship of Christ. They must be continually and constantly evaluated and placed upon the altar of sacrifice. Some are like weights that we must let go and give over to God. Others are like obstacles we confront in our ascent up the mountain. As you read the list ask the Holy Spirit to show you what areas of your life need to be placed upon the altar and consumed. These are ten of the most common areas of life that if not given proper priority consistently and repeatedly compete for your allegiance and can often distract you from a relationship with Christ. They must be offered on the altar of sacrifice.

Ten Life Distractions that Compete for Your Allegiance

1.   Personal Dreams

Dreams are anything you hope and desire to have, be or accomplish in your life. Dreams and the desire for accomplishment and impact in life are given to us by God but can

> *Now He cries "Come up!"*
> *and there we stand, between*
> *us and the foot of the*
> *mountain is an altar.*

easily become a god unto themselves. If your dreams and aspirations come first in your life then they will be a constant source of conflict in your relationship with God, and as a result, God will take a distant second in your life.

> *But seek first His kingdom and His righteousness, and all*
> *these things will be added to you.*
> *Matthew 6:33*

2.   Finances

The Bible speaks to great extent about money and possessions and for good reason. There are only two types of possessions in this world: those you own and those that own you. If you can't let it go then you've got an idol that rules you. The Scriptures say the love of money is the root of all evil (1 Tim. 6:10). Now notice, it's not money but the love of money that is the root of all evil. The Bible makes a bold claim that money is the root of ALL evil. How is that possible? The problem of money, or more specifically what money can do—is at its most fundamental level it provides a false sense of security and temporary happiness that lulls a person into believing with money they don't need God. The reality is the most important things in life, peace of mind, hope, love, salvation, just to name a few, try as we might, cannot be purchased.

If your love of money surpasses your love of God then money is your God. If you see a person in need and are prompted by God to give them money or to buy something to give them and you disobey because you don't want to release the money then money is an idol. If you are at church and tip God rather than tithe when the offering is received you better evaluate your heart. Many believers are poor and living far below what God intends because they are not practicing generosity and sowing into the Kingdom of God. Open up your hand and release your finances as the Lord directs and He will then be able to fill your open hand that was once clutched tight.

3.   Physical Health

In good health and poor health we are to offer our bodies as living sacrifices holy and acceptable unto God (Rom. 12:1,2). The Scriptures also declare our bodies are a temple for the abiding presence of God (1 Jn. 2:27). Don't make your body an idol and don't abuse and neglect it either.

4.   Family

Our children and family are gifts from the Lord. As parents we are to raise them up and teach them to love and obey God through our example as well as speech.

> It is only when He is Lord of your life that you will have the power to love and lead your family as unto the Lord.

Raising family is a tremendous responsibility that can pull us in a dozen different directions and leave us feeling stretched to our breaking point. We must constantly place our family and our own efforts at the feet of Jesus. It is only when He is Lord of your life that you will have the power to love and lead your family as unto the Lord.

5.   *Will*

In a time of great need, Jesus understood the sacrifice of will when he cried out to His Father in the garden, *"Not my will but Yours be done."* (Lk. 22:42) Our will, our sense of self autonomy, personal authority and decision making must always come second to God's will for our life. When you would rather do it your way knowing good and well it's not the will of your Father or don't care to stop and seek His guidance then it's time to repent and lay your will on the altar of sacrifice.

6.   *Marriage*

God empowers us to love our spouse in good times and in hard times. He commands the man to love his wife as Christ loves the church and to lay down his life for her. He commands the woman to love her husband and submit to his authority as unto the Lord. (Eph. 5:22-25) This kind of love between a husband and a wife is only possible when Christ is first in their individual lives and at the center of the marriage. When our spouse comes before God then they are an idol. When they lead us away from Christ, then they are a distraction. When we pursue and nurture a marriage relationship, as noble as that sounds, at the expense of a personal relationship with God then the marriage becomes a weight that separates us from the Father. It is only in communion and intimacy in Christ that we are empowered to love our spouse as God commands.

It is only in communion and intimacy in Christ that we are empowered to love our spouse as God commands.

7.   *Career*

A Career can offer stability, prestige, identity and accomplishment; all good and healthy in their own right. But when we pursue our career before Christ it becomes an idol to us. When we sacrifice and neglect our spouse or our children or the House of God so we can advance our career then we must reevaluate our commitments. The Bible tells us what does it profit a man to gain the whole world yet lose his own soul? How is that job or career path going to console you when you get there and you lose your wife and children? Listen to your spouse and to the needs of your family. The children only grow up once and how can you love your spouse as unto the Lord if you're never around or too busy and distracted when you are?

8. Time

Twenty-four hours, it's all we get no matter who we are. Life is made up of the stuff and we value our time greatly, especially our free time. When we spend our time more often doing something we want rather than what God has asked of us then we haven't surrendered our time to God.

9. Pet Sins

Concerning pet sins a pastor once said, "Little rattle snakes grow up to be big rattle snakes." Pet sins are ungodly habits and lifestyle choices we haven't surrendered over to God and continue to practice even though we know they are sin and keeping us from experiencing the full life God has for us. They are often done in secret or only with certain people or in certain contexts. They are sins of the flesh we still enjoy too much to give up. Examples of pet sins may include gossiping, watching inappropriate movies or television shows, smoking, gluttony, cursing, overspending, laziness, etc... Pet sins are like small leaks in a tire that seem small and insignificant but are constantly draining your spiritual life. In time these pin holes become entry points for the activity of the devil and they grow into gashes that steal, kill and destroy in every area of your life.

Pet sins are like small leaks in a tire that seem small and insignificant but are constantly draining your spiritual life. In time these pin holes become entry points for the activity of the devil.

10. Pride

Pride is a self satisfaction and sense of independence based on personal accomplishment that then compares itself to others for the purpose of personal satisfaction often at the expense of others. Simply put, pride is when we love ourselves more than God and others. The Apostle John warned us to beware of the pride of life:

> For all that is in the world, the lust of the flesh and the lust of the eyes and the boastful pride of life, is not from the Father, but is from the world.
>
> 1 John 2:16

Pride was responsible for the birth of sin into the universe God created when it is said pride entered the heart of Lucifer and he attempted to overthrow the Kingdom of God in Heaven. Later in his fallen state on earth he appealed to the self autonomy of Eve in the Garden of Eden by questioning what God had said to her. By questioning the character of God and His clear prohibition to touching the Tree of the Knowledge of Good and Evil he was in fact stimulating her pride and sense of independence apart from her creator. Satan fell to pride and from then on has used pride as his number one tactic to seduce humanity to join him in rebellion. God resists the proud but gives grace to the humble (James 4:6). The two most obvious fruits of pride are arrogance and unteachableness. Beware when you see these fruit in your life. Pray the Holy Spirit to pluck them from your life and cast them on the altar of sacrifice for when left to mature they lead to spiritual blindness and separation from God.

The two most obvious fruits of pride are arrogance and unteachableness. Beware when you see these fruit in your life.

Most mountaineers will find the need to lay any one of the above ten areas on the altar of sacrifice. These areas of life constantly compete for supremacy and must be repeatedly offered up to God for only through His grace and empowerment are we able to resist. As we continue the habit of reflection and activity of exposing these areas of our life through the guiding of the Holy Spirit we will preparing our hearts, or better, the Holy Spirit will be preparing our hearts to ascend into the presence of a holy God. Once our hearts are clean before Him and we have sacrificed the sins that so easily beset, then it opens our spiritual ears to answer the call of God to Come Hear!

Come Hear!

Then Moses came and recounted to the people all the words of the LORD and all the ordinances; and all the people answered with one voice and said, "All the words which the LORD has spoken we will do!"

Exodus 24:3

Then He said to Moses,…

Exodus 24:1

Then God said, "Let there be light"; and there was light.

Genesis 1:3

Moreover, the sound of the wings of the cherubim was heard as far as the outer court, like the voice of God Almighty when He speaks.

Ezekiel 10:5

Your word is a lamp to my feet and a light to my path.

Psalms 119:105

and the sheep follow him because they know his voice.

John 10:2-4

4

Direction

Then Moses came and recounted to the people all the words of the LORD and all the ordinances; and all the people answered with one voice and said, "All the words which the LORD has spoken we will do!"

Exodus 24:3

E ffective communication is vital between climbers and guides as they navigate up a mountain. Lose contact with your guide and the consequences can be fatal! As you follow God up the mountain He invites you to listen and pay careful attention to His guidance and direction. In your ascent God gives you two primary modes, or ways to hear Him speak to you. One, The Holy Bible, or in context of spiritual mountaineering we can also call, the Climber's Guidebook. And two, His still small inner voice. Both modes of communication, the Bible and His voice, are essential to developing a strong and healthy relationship with God and are required for receiving His direction and guidance to live the life He has destined for you.

Before we delve into the specifics of how God talks to you, it's important for you to understand that God created you for fellowship with Him and that your relationship with Him is built around communication. The spirit that God placed within you allows you to connect and talk with a spiritual God. One of the most amazing realities about God is that He wants a dynamic and exciting relationship with you! That is one of the main reasons, perhaps the main reason, He created you in His image and likeness. Your inborn ability to connect with a supernatural God is no accident. Let's now look in the Bible at some of the many ways and examples God interacted with His children. This should encourage and inspire you to always be listening for His voice because as you're about to see, our God is a talker!

Our God is a Talker!

From the very beginning of the Bible, in the very first chapter, we see that our God is a talker! Ten times in Genesis 1, the phrase, "God said", is used. 255 times in the Bible the phrase. "*The word of the Lord*" is used. Throughout the Old Testament is recorded example after example of God initiating and talking to people, beginning with Adam and Eve in the garden. Even after the fall, when Adam and Eve sinned and disobeyed His instruction, God did not stop talking. (Gen. 3) He warned Cain that sin was crouching at the door of his heart and desired to have him. (Gen. 4) Enoch had such a wonderful relationship with God that God took him to Heaven without seeing death: "*Enoch walked with God; and he was not, for God took him.*". (Gen. 5:24)

Even when the downward spiral of sin gripped the heart of all mankind and utterly blackened it in wickedness, God did not give up or stop talking. He searched and found a righteous man, Noah, and told him to build an ark to save himself and his family. (Gen. 6-9)

It is with the advent of Abraham that we really begin to see into the heart and desire of God to raise up a people for His own possession. (Gen. 12) He established a covenant with Abraham and his descendants and ratified the covenant with His very Presence passing between the animal sacrifice as a smoking oven and flaming torch. (Gen. 15) He continued His active role with Abraham and then carried that to his sons, Isaac and Jacob. He even wrestled with Jacob and gave him a new name and a new identity, Israel. (Gen. 32) Israel had 12 sons, one of which was Joseph, who God spoke to him through dreams and visions. (Gen. 37) The life of Joseph was an amazing demonstration of the providence of God upon a person and it covers the last thirteen chapters of Genesis. (Gen. 37-50) Through his life God provided a means by which Israel's entire family could move to Egypt and escape a severe famine.

Over 400 pass while living in Egypt and Israel's posterity grew from a clan of 70 to a nation of perhaps a million or more. But they are a nation of slaves. They had flourished in Goshen, the land given to them by Pharaoh to dwell in, but at some point the Egyptians felt their Hebrew guests had outgrown their welcome and feared they would grow beyond containment. So in response to their fears, the Egyptians appointed taskmasters over the Hebrews and subjected them to servitude and hard labor. (Ex. 1)

While Moses was herding sheep on the backside of the desert, God appeared to him as a flame that did not consume the bush. He told Moses He had heard the cries and misery of the Hebrews and commissioned Moses to be their redeemer. Through Divine instruction, guidance and supernatural miracles over the natural world, Moses rescued the Hebrews from the Egyptians and delivered them to the foot of Mt. Sinai.

Moses developed a fascinating relationship with God. He would enter into the Tent of Meeting, a temporary Tabernacle where the Ark of the Covenant was kept, and talk to God face to face as a man talks to another man. Read the fascinating account recorded in Exodus:

> *Whenever Moses entered the tent, the pillar of cloud would descend and stand at the entrance of the tent; and the LORD would speak with Moses. When all the people saw the pillar of cloud standing at the entrance of the tent, all the people would arise and worship, each at the entrance of his tent. Thus the LORD used to speak to Moses face to face, just as a man speaks to his friend.*
>
> *Exodus 33:9-11*

As a result of these conversations and encounters with God a fascinating effect occurred. They caused his face to literally glow!

> But whenever Moses went in before the LORD to speak with Him, he would take off the veil until he came out; and whenever he came out and spoke to the sons of Israel what he had been commanded, the sons of Israel would see the face of Moses, that the skin of Moses' face shone. So Moses would replace the veil over his face until he went in to speak with Him.
>
> Exodus 34:34-35

Moses' glowing face was a natural manifestation of a supernatural encounter. But if seen through the lens of the New Testament, we have a very clear spiritual truth: Talking to God and spending time in His presence, has an effect—it changes you and makes you more like Christ!

In the books of Joshua and Judges, God continued to engage and talk with men and women like Joshua, Gideon, Debra and Samson. Then He called a young boy as he slept and began a life long relationship with Samuel. Samuel understood obedience and the value of God talking. The Bible says he *"let none of his words fail"*. (1 Sam. 3:19) In other words, Samuel paid very close attention when God talked to him and was careful to obey every word.

Samuel eventually grew to a man, becoming one of the premier prophets in the Old Testament era. He ushered in the age of the kings by anointing the first two kings of Israel: Saul, of the tribe of Benjamin, and David, of the tribe of Judah.

Moses' glowing face was a natural manifestation to a supernatural encounter but if seen through the lens of the New Testament we have a very clear spiritual truth: Talking to God, spending time in His presence has an effect; it changes you, makes you more like Christ!

King Saul fell from grace and his anointing from God to rule was lifted. God then instructed the prophet Samuel to anoint David to be the next king of Israel. At David's prophetic inauguration, the Spirit of God came mightily upon David from that day forward:

> *Then Samuel took the horn of oil and anointed him in the midst of his brothers; and the Spirit of the LORD came mightily upon David from that day forward...*
>
> *1 Samuel 16:13*

King David penned much of the book of Psalms under the anointing and presence of God.

Solomon, David's son, succeeded his father as king of Israel. God appeared to Solomon and bestowed him with wisdom and leadership that also included great riches and wealth. (1 Kings 3)

It is during the age of the kings that the prophet Elijah rose to prominence. One of his most famous prophetic acts is recorded in 1 Kings 18 when he challenged the 450 false prophets of baal to a call-fire-from-heaven showdown. God answered Elijah's prayer and consumed the altar with fire from the sky. Elijah purified the nation of idolatry by striking down with the sword all 450 false prophets. He expected a mighty revival but instead incurred the wrath and a death sentence from the wicked Queen Jezebel.

The prophet Elijah, fearing for his life, ran from Jezebel and hid in a cave. It is here God speaks to him not in the fire or earthquake, but in a still quiet whisper. Elijah needed the comfort of knowing he was not alone and that God was very close, as close as a whisper. (1 Kings 19) Later at the end of Elijah's earthly tenure God brought a chariot of fire down and whisked him to Heaven. (2 Kings 2)

In the rebellious and idolatrous years of Israel, when they had forsaken God, disobeyed his commands and worshipped foreign gods, God did not stop talking. It was during this time He sent prophets such as Daniel, Ezekiel, Jeremiah, Jonah, Micah, Nahum, and many others with messages of repentance that often began with, *"Thus says* the LORD." God always had something to say. If the people didn't listen He would raise up a prophet to deliver His message. Actually, God talks so much that it's odd or unusual if He's silent. The four hundred years between the last book of the Old Testament, Malachi, and the beginning of the New Testament is called the "Silent Years" because there was no prophet of God delivering His message. Our God has always been a talker.

Jesus is the Message

The single greatest revelation and example of the desire of God to talk and communicate with us was in the sending of His son, Jesus Christ. It is from the pages of the Gospels, in the life and ministry of Christ, that we have the clearest expression of the heart and message of God. Notice what Jesus said about His purpose and message as recorded in John 17:

> Now they have come to know that everything You have given Me is from You; for the words which You gave Me I have given to them; and they received them and truly understood that I came forth from You, and they believed that You sent Me.
>
> John 17:7-8

It is from the pages of Gospels, in the life and ministry of Christ, we get the clearest expression of the heart and message of God to us.

Jesus made it clear God the Father gave Him His message to deliver to the people. When Jesus is speaking, God is speaking. If you want to know what God is saying you need to look no further than Jesus. The life, death and resurrection of Christ was THE message God wanted to deliver to you. His desire to restore you to a right status with Him in order to enjoy fellowship with Him required that your sin issue be accounted for. The greatest message God has sent to you is found in the most quoted and familiar verse in the Bible, John 3:16:

For God so loved the world, that He gave His only begotten Son, that whoever believes in Him shall not perish, but have eternal life.

John 3:16

God did not stop talking after the resurrection of Christ. He was just getting warmed up. In Acts 2, the Holy Spirit descended upon the 120 in the upper room and filled their mouths with unknown languages and messages of repentance to all nations, creeds, races and languages. It was like the Tower of Babel in reverse. If you remember in Genesis 11, the people decided to unite and build a tower to heaven, the first attempt at a one world government, and God came down and confused their languages and spread them out over the face of the earth. Here in Acts 2, the evidence of the Holy Spirit in the disciples was speaking in unknown foreign languages. It was a supernatural event to produce a supernatural result. The Holy Spirit spoke through the disciples to unite all peoples, races and nations, not under a one world manmade government, but to unite them under one Kingdom, the Kingdom of God.

Now as a New Testament believer, post-resurrection, post-Pentecost, not only do you have the Bible as the words of God to look to for guidance and direction, but now you are a carrier of the anointing! You have the Holy Spirit within you to teach you everything you need to know and guide you up the mountain of Zion!

As for you, the anointing which you received from Him abides in you, and you have no need for anyone to teach you; but as His anointing teaches you about all things, and is true and is not a lie, and just as it has taught you, you abide in Him.

1 John 2:27

53

God Never Stopped Calling

Not only do we see God talking from the very first chapter of Genesis, He is still talking and inviting us into His presence. In the last book and chapter of the Bible, Revelation 22, He is still calling:

> The Spirit and the bride say, "Come." And let the one who hears say, "Come." And let the one who is thirsty come; let the one who wishes take the water of life without cost.
> Revelation 22:17

You can memorize the whole Bible and it do you no good. During Jesus' time the Scribes and Pharisees had memorized much of the Torah-the first five books of the Old Testament, but they still couldn't recognize Jesus the Messiah standing right in front of them.

He continued to talk throughout the history of mankind and He continues to speak and invite those who will listen today.

How can I know when God is talking to me?

Now that we know God is a talker and desires to engage us and interact for fellowship and guidance the next question becomes, "How does God speak?" or more specifically, "How can I know when God is talking to me?" Since the bedrock foundation of a relationship with God is communication, it is vitally important to know how God speaks to us. At the beginning of this chapter, I shared that there are two primary ways God speaks to us. First, the Holy Bible. And second, His inner voice. Let's first explore how God speaks through His written Word, the Bible.

The Mountaineer Handbook

All Scripture is inspired by God and profitable for teaching, for reproof, for correction, for training in righteousness; so that the man of God may be adequate, equipped for every good work.

2 Timothy 3:16-17

It is from God's written Word you can know God and learn to experience His Presence. The Bible is His supernatural revelation to man and is profitable for many things. The Bible is your manual and guide on the mountain of Zion. It is your mountaineer handbook.

If we believe we have received a word or impression from God and it is in conflict with the Holy Bible then we have misunderstood God's voice for something else.

Consider your Bible one of the primary ways God speaks and it is the ultimate authority to measure all thoughts, impressions and leadings you feel you have received from God. God cannot lie and will not speak or direct you to say or do anything contrary to His written Word. If you believe you have received a word or impression from God and it is in conflict with the Holy Bible, then you have misunderstood God's voice for something or someone else.

As you read His Word, God will often highlight or illuminate a portion of Scripture that He wants to communicate. Let me explain. Do you know you can memorize the whole Bible and it do you no good? You can also faithfully read through the Bible year after year and it have no effect on your life. During Jesus' time the Scribes and Pharisees had memorized much of the Torah-the first five books of the Old Testament, but they were still unable to recognize Jesus the Messiah standing right in front of them! How is this even possible? The Apostle Paul hints at this tragic possibility in 2 Corinthians:

who also made us adequate as servants of a new covenant, not of the letter but of the Spirit; for the letter kills, but the Spirit gives life.

2 Corinthians 3:6

Under the Old Covenant man was required to follow the letter of the law. The emphasis was on doing and obedience to a set of rules. But as Apostle Paul stated, following the letter of the law led to death. The law eventually suffocated any and every person under the weight of their inadequacy and failure to keep it all. But you are now living under a new covenant! The New Covenant is based on the Spirit who wrote the words of the New Testament. The New Covenant's foundation is not in rules but in relationship. It is listening to the person of the Holy Spirit speaking the words on the pages of the Bible that lead to life.

As you read and study God's Word you must be led by the Spirit and watch for His inspiration and revelation. What this often looks like for me is I'll be reading a portion of Scripture and then a verse or phrase will seem to jump off the page at me. At that moment, I'll instantly and deeply feel and hear God saying to stop and read no further. I'll then go back and reread and meditate on that portion of Scripture that I feel the Holy Spirit is drawing me to and then look and listen for His voice and direction. I always read my Bible with the expectancy and faith of knowing and waiting for God to pull me in to a verse or Biblical thought that He has been waiting to show me.

Guided by His Voice

The second way God speaks to us is through His Spirit. There are many ways the Holy Spirit uses to get our attention, such as through people, life experiences, night dreams, and the Bible. The Bible is unique in that it is God's ultimate standard and measuring device for comparing every other message we believe we have received from God.

Although the Holy Spirit uses many ways to get our attention-I like to call them invitations, He primarily uses two ways to communicate: through an inner voice and through impressions.

Just as you have been given your natural senses of sight, smell, touch, hearing and smelling to navigate and communicate with the natural world, so God has given you spiritual or supernatural, senses that correspond with your natural senses to navigate and communicate with the spiritual world. These supernatural senses allow you to relate, worship and communicate with a supernatural God. The Apostle John says it in this way:

> *"God is spirit, and those who worship Him must worship in spirit and truth."*
>
> *John 4:24*

When the Apostle John says "God is spirit" he is simply saying God is supernatural. He is not of this natural world which He created, He is totally other or beyond and above the natural realm. He has deposited a spirit within you to make it possible for you to relate, communicate and be in fellowship with Him.

So let's get back to your spiritual senses. Just as your natural senses are connected and a part of your natural body, so your spiritual senses are connected and a part of your spirit. In other words, your spirit, which is the supernatural dimension deposited within you by God, gives you the capacity to see, hear, feel, taste and smell the supernatural, or spiritual world. Once you understand and embrace that reality it opens up a whole other world of capabilities and realities. God is able to increase His revelation and instruction to you as you are more in tune, or more sensitive, to His supernatural ways of communication. It's similar to radio or T.V. stations in that they are broadcasting and sending signals out all the time, but without a radio or television to capture and transmit the signal you are unable to receive the message. Another way to see it is that many understand and have been taught to listen to the voice of God, that inner voice, but that's just one channel on the television. God doesn't just speak but He also shows and gives impressions through our other spiritual senses. He wants you to increase the channels on your spiritual antennae!

The Inner Voice of the Spirit

Learning to recognize the voice of God when He speaks to you is vital to a healthy and growing relationship. You can be confident you can *hear* His voice because Jesus said so in the Gospel of John:

> *My sheep hear My voice, and I know them, and they follow Me;*
>
> *John 10:27*

You can also be confident to *know* and *recognize* His voice when He speaks to you :

> *When he puts forth all his own, he goes ahead of them, and the sheep follow him because they know his voice.*
>
> *John 10:4*

What confidence you can have in hearing and knowing the voice of God when He speaks to you! As you grow in fellowship and spend time in His presence, you will become more and more intimately familiar with His voice and be able to distinguish it from your own thoughts or from the lies of Satan. Don't stress out if it is difficult for you to recognize when God speaks to you. One of the key marks of maturity is a keen familiarity with the voice of God and that only comes by spending time in His presence.

The Impressions of the Holy Spirit

Hearing the inner voice of the Holy Spirit engages your spiritual ears. But as I've said, God does more than talking to communicate to us. Let's begin with the spiritual eyes God has given you to see what He is saying and doing.

A good example of spiritual vision is recorded in John 5:19. In this passage Jesus gives us a priceless glimpse into how He communicated with His Father. Jesus said He would see what His Father was doing and He knew that was His invitation to do likewise:

Ascending the Mountain of God

Therefore Jesus answered and was saying to them, "Truly, truly, I say to you, the Son can do nothing of Himself, unless it is something He sees the Father doing; for whatever the Father does, these things the Son also does in like manner.

John 5:19

According to Thayer's Greek dictionary the word "sees" in John 5:19 is the word *blepo* in Greek. It has a literal meaning 'to see with the bodily eye.' But I don't believe that is what Jesus meant when He said He saw the activity of His Father, because according to Colossians 1:15 and 1 Timothy 1:17, God is invisible. *Blepo* also can metaphorically mean 'to discern mentally, observe, perceive, discover, and understand.' In other words, Jesus saw with His eyes of faith the activity of His Father. You also have been given eyes of faith to see the activity of the Heavenly Father, and when you discern His activity it is also an invitation for you to *"do in like manner."*

If God wants to open our physical eyes to see into the supernatural realm, He surely can. An excellent example of that is found in 2 Kings 6 when the Prophet Elisha asked God to open the natural eyes of his attendant to see the supernatural armies of angels around them. Although that is possible—the Bible overflows with examples of those who saw angels and the Lord with their natural eyes—it is the exception rather than the norm. The majority of the time God opens our spiritual eyes through our thoughts or imaginations.

Let me give you a couple of personal examples from my own life to illustrate. Early on in my own spiritual growth journey I was listening to a minister, whom I had just met, share his personal testimony. As he was speaking, I was imagining him on a television talk show being interviewed and sharing his testimony. I thought it was my own mind "wandering" until, after he was finished another minister spoke up and prophesied that God was going to take his testimony to the nations through television. It was then I began to understand that it was not my own thoughts but God was speaking to me through my spiritual eyes.

As I have grown in my faith eyes, what I like to call my spiritual seeing, I pay close attention to my imaginations when I am in the Spirit or ministering to others. During a prayer service I had the privilege of praying for a young lady, and as soon as I laid hands on her I saw a jungle full of wild animals. I then asked the Holy Spirit what this meant and I heard him say He was calling her to be a missionary to Africa. That is one example of seeing and hearing God communicate through the imagination.

Another way God often communicates to us is through our spiritual sense of touch, or feeling and impressions. This is one way God communicates that can be often overlooked because it does directly involve or affect our natural sensations. In this mode of spiritual communication we can sense God's communication in a number of ways. For example, have you ever been in a situation, perhaps meeting a person, where something just didn't feel right? Or you were about to make a decision or do something important and you had a check, or warning pause, or a knot in your stomach, within your spirit? It was not something you heard or saw but more of a feeling. Other times we get what's often called "spiritual goose bumps" when in the presence of God. The hair may rise up on our arms or neck and we get flushed or feel heat radiating through a part of our body. These manifestations in and of themselves are only evidence of God, they are not the communication or the message God wants to deliver. Some people like to call these moments intuition or a sixth sense but more likely they are God's way of supernaturally speaking to us. If this happens to you, get in the habit of asking God, "What are you trying to show me?"

God is always talking, through His Word and His Spirit, and always inviting you to join Him

Each time we can see past the veil, look beyond the natural event and see with our spiritual eyes Him at work or hear His voice with our spiritual ears, they are royal invitations, a special assignment, sent directly from the King of the Mountain to join Him.

in conversation and Kingdom activity. Each time you see past the veil, look beyond the natural event and see with your spiritual eyes Him at work or hear His voice with your spiritual ears. They are royal invitations, a special assignment, sent directly to you from the King of the Mountain. Often those royal invitations are time sensitive and require a step out in faith. Just as they are seen by faith, so they must be acted on by faith. They may come at any time of the day or the night, and usually require an interruption of our agenda. It wasn't until Moses turned aside to go see the bush that was burning and not consumed that God spoke to Him from the fire. May your response to His voice be like that of the people when Moses read to them the words of God:

> *and all the people answered with one voice and said, "All the words which the LORD has spoken we will do!"*
> *Exodus 24:3*

When you grow in maturity and become wise and sensitive to the guidance and direction from the Holy Spirit, it builds your confidence to know He has spoken. That confidence is vital for the next station on the mountain, when God calls you to move in obedience and Come On!

Come On!

Then Moses went up with Aaron, Nadab and Abihu, and seventy of the elders of Israel,

Exodus 24:9

Then Hezekiah said, "Now that you have consecrated yourselves to the LORD, come near...

2 Chronicles 29:31

Draw near to God and He will draw near to you. Cleanse your hands, you sinners; and purify your hearts, you double-minded.

James 4:8

Then the King will say to those on His right, 'Come, you who are blessed of My Father, inherit the kingdom prepared for you from the foundation of the world.

Matthew 25:34

The Spirit and the bride say, "Come." And let the one who hears say, "Come." And let the one who is thirsty come; let the one who wishes take the water of life without cost.

Revelation 22:17

"When Christ calls a man, He bids him come and die."

Dietrich Bonhoeffer, The Cost of Discipleship

5

Mobilization

M ovement is one characteristic that separates life from non-life. Your heart beats to pump and move vital oxygen rich blood throughout your body. Still water will eventually stagnate. A water-soaked sponge left sitting in the sink too long will soon sour and stink. Sit too long at an intersection when a red light has turned green and you're going to get honked at. You have been given the green light to pursue God up the mountain. You cannot stay where you are and go with God. What are you waiting for? C'mon, it's time to move! HONK!

Then Moses went up... Exodus 24:9

Moses wasted no time in responding to the call of God and neither should you. The devil's playground is procrastination. Procrastination is nothing more than delayed obedience. When you are slow to respond to the direction of the Holy Spirit it creates a foothold, a base of operations, for the devil. Delayed obedience gives the devil permission and time to kill, steal and destroy all the muster and energy you had to begin the climb.

You are as Close to God as You Choose to Be

James gives us a powerful truth concerning our responsibility in the drawing near to God:

> Come near to God, and he will come near to you.
>
> James 4:8

James was not writing to unbelievers when he said to come near to God, he was addressing his brothers and sisters in the Lord. When you were a sinner you were blinded and lost to the things of God and He moved towards you first. Jesus made that clear in the Gospel of John when He said, *"No man can come to me, except the Father which hath sent me draw him"* (Jn. 6:44a) But now you are a part of the family of God and have been placed at the foot of the mountain of God. He pursued you with a relentless love and saved you from the path of destruction you were heading down. Now it is time for you to pursue Christ! Respond to His love and grace He has so richly poured out into your life and draw near to God! He promises if you come up the mountain He will come down and meet you.

The reason there are few spiritual giants walking the earth today is there are too few willing to forsake all and come near to God.

Do you realize you are as close to God as you choose to be? You can't blame your tepid or flat relationship with God on anyone but yourself. Your spouse isn't to blame, or your job, or your health, or your church, or anything or anyone else. And you surely can't blame God for a cold passionless heart towards Him. He has supremely demonstrated His love and desire for you and is waiting to reward you with His presence the moment you move in His direction.

Many Want the Glory But Don't Know the Story

To lose yourself in God you must first lose yourself. Life in God mandates death to self. Dietrich Bonhoeffer, a Christian martyr who died at the order of Hitler during the Nazi regime understood the cost of movement and obedience when he penned in his book, The Cost of Discipleship, "When God calls a man, he bids him come and die." The reason there are few spiritual giants walking the earth today is there are too few willing to forsake all and come near to God.

The Apostle Paul was caught up into the third heaven and shown *"inexpressible things, things that man is not permitted to tell."* (2 Cor. 12:4) Wouldn't you like to have times with God like that! Before you shout "Yes, Lord!" there was a price Paul paid for that privilege. He shared some of his tribulations and sacrifices in a letter to the church at Corinth. As you read the following account of Paul's suffering and trials ask yourself, how much would *you* endure for the cause of Christ? How much would you sacrifice to receive supernatural revelations from God?

> *Many want the glory they see on godly men and women but they don't know their story; the price they pay everyday for that intimacy and power from God.*

> *Are they servants of Christ?--I speak as if insane--I more so; in far more labors, in far more imprisonments, beaten times without number, often in danger of death. Five times I received from the Jews thirty-nine lashes. Three times I was beaten with rods, once I was stoned, three times I was shipwrecked, a night and a day I have spent in the deep. I have been on frequent journeys, in dangers from rivers, dangers from robbers, dangers from my countrymen, dangers from the Gentiles, dangers in the city, dangers in the wilderness, dangers on the sea, dangers among false brethren; I have been in labor and hardship, through many sleepless nights, in hunger and thirst, often without food, in cold and exposure. Apart from such external things, there is the daily pressure on me of concern for all the churches.*
> *2 Corinthians 11:23-28*

When your testimony begins to compare to that of Paul then no doubt you too will experience visions and encounters with God not meant for human ears. Many want the glory they see on godly men and women but they don't know their story; the price they pay everyday for that intimacy and power from God.

What's Your Excuse?

Life pulls on us from a dozen different directions. There's always someone or something demanding our time and attention. When it comes to spending time with God, that demand also weighs in on us. The thing about God is He isn't a bully or pushy when it comes to time with Him. He's always there and when we are open and sensitive to Him we hear His call. But we can ignore and refuse His invitations up the mountain too. There's always an excuse to start tomorrow; and tomorrow turns into next week and next week into next month and next month turns into next year. Before long our excuses have robbed us of countless mountain top experiences and we are left feeling empty and distant. Our Savior feels to us more like a stepdad we visit on holidays rather than a full-time devoted father we see every day. God forgive us! We have abused His gentleness and let the bossy demands of everyday life drown out His still small voice.

It's time to lay hold of the calling, rejecting all excuses and pursue Him regardless of the cost. You should no longer acquiesce to the mundane demands of life but instead rise up and grab hold of that for which Christ Jesus has grabbed hold of you! It's an upward call, so climb! (Phil. 4:14) It's time to move forward and fight and defend, without excuse, your time on the mountain top.

You are called to move! There is no better time to pursue Jesus and ascend the mountain than right now. Begin the ascent today. The following are five excuses that stall believers in the valley and keep them from the mountain top and how to avoid them.

1. *Begin the Ascent Even if the Timing is Not Right.*

In John chapter two Jesus and his disciples were invited to a wedding in Cana. Jewish weddings in Biblical times were often week long affairs full of feasting and festivities. Grand banquets were prepared for many family, friends, neighbors and important guests and the week was spent celebrating the new life of the married couple. Often the whole town was invited to the wedding and it was considered an insult to refuse an invitation.

No indication is given that Jesus and the disciples were there to preach or evangelize, they were celebrating along with the people. But the wine ran out and the mother of Jesus turned to her son for a solution. Jesus' replied to his mother clearly and communicated he had not come to solve any problems or perform a miracle. He response to her was, *"Woman, what does that have to do with us? My hour has not yet come." (Jn. 2:4)* It seems that Mary took the wedding party's problem to heart and was compelled to help them to avoid embarrassment. Perhaps Mary was related in someway and had a special interest in their predicament. Regardless, her son's response to her request was a flat refusal. But not deterred by the lack of interest from her son to do anything about the shortage of wine, she immediately turned to the servants and said, *"Whatever He says to you, do it.". (Jn. 2:5)* Jesus then ordered the servants to fill six stone water pots, each 20 or 30 gallons, to the brim with water and draw some to take to the headwaiter. Between the time they were filled and the time the headwaiter placed the cup to his mouth God had supernaturally transformed the water into wine!

Not a likely place or time to perform a miracle. Jesus' first miracle was not in the synagogue or big auditorium. It wasn't during an altar call or after an anointed teaching. It seems Jesus hadn't even seen His Father showing Him that was the day He was going to reveal His glory through His first supernatural act. It was kind of an unlikely time and place, a wedding feast. But Jesus discerned in the moment it was time,

He recognized His Father at work and joined Him accordingly. Jesus did not let "bad" timing keep Him from obedience.

You will never find the perfect time or place to begin the strenuous journey of mountain climbing into the glory cloud. Don't let less than perfect situations keep you from pressing in to His presence. You'll discover, just like Jesus did, that when you move in obedience even if the timing isn't right you will shift the atmosphere and release miracles. Jesus was not only the Bread of Life but He is also the Life of the party!

2. Begin the Ascent Even if you have a lot of Problems.

Careful planning was needed to accommodate so many wedding guests. To run out of wine was an embarrassment to the family and broke the unwritten rule of hospitality. They had a big problem on their hands. The reputation of the entire family was at stake. This shortage of wine was much more serious than you might think.

Will you pursue Him in spite of your problems? It's easy to plan a quiet time and spend time in prayer when everything is going smooth and your schedule is wide open. But the kind of tenacity God is looking for is when we must struggle and defend our mountain ascents in the face of great adversity. It's important to realize that all the miracles and opportunities for God to show Himself mighty in the Bible happened because there was a problem. Don't let your problems become obstacles that keep you from His Presence. Press in and press up in the midst of your problems. See them for what they can be, opportunities for God to do the miraculous in your life.

You'll discover, just like Jesus did, that when you move in obedience even if the timing isn't right you will shift the atmosphere and release miracles.

Daniel, Shadrack, Meshack, and Abednigo in the book of Daniel are good examples of having a lot of problems. They were prisoners in a foreign country and asked to bow down and worship an idle. The penalty for refusing was execution by fire. Now there's a problem! But because of their obedience at the risk of their very lives they encountered a mighty miracle and beheld the Son of God among them in the fire! (Dan. 3)

3.   Begin the Ascent Even if you Don't Feel Like It..

"My hour has not yet come". (Jn. 2:4) Not exactly what we might have expected Jesus to say. Jesus was about 30 years old and at the beginning of his ministry. He had not performed any miracles up to this point. He clearly communicated the time was not right but He honored the request of His mother anyway. As you learned from chapter four, Jesus only did what He saw the Father doing. (Jn. 5:19) In that moment after his mother's request he surely must have petitioned His Father and saw that

Spiritual maturity is not measured by Sundays in the pew but by hours on the mountain.

the Father was ready to perform a miracle. He was so in tune to His Father that even after the request of His mother He was checking in and listening to see what He was to do. In that moment, even though He went to the wedding feast with the standing orders to not perform any miracle, He was sensitive enough to the leading of the Holy Spirit to know His standing orders had been changed. He was to respond in obedience to the request of His mother because He saw His Father was at work.

His obedience to the Father was not based on past feelings or past orders but on a dynamic in the moment sensitivity to the will of His Father. It is no different for us. We do not obey God based on how we personally feel about the situation. Your feelings will lie to you. We are to pursue God up the mountain and walk in faithfulness and obedience regardless of how we feel. We are not commanded to be feeling led but rather to be Spirit led. Some of the greatest times I have had in the presence of God were when I pressed in and pursued Him when I didn't feel like it. Some of the most powerful revelations and wisdom gems from Heaven came when I forced myself and pressed past fleshly inadequacies. God has special rewards from Heaven reserved for those who take the mountain by force. You are called to pursue God whether you feel like it or not. Don't let your feelings get in the way of a mighty move of God.

> *God has special rewards from Heaven reserved for those who take the mountain by force.*

4. Begin the Ascent Even if you Don't Feel Qualified.

The servants did not know Jesus but they obeyed His unusual request. They did not ask questions or complain. The scripture simply says they immediately did what Jesus told them to do.

It is a fact, the longer you know Jesus and have a relationship with Him the closer and stronger your faith in him becomes. No matter, don't let a young relationship with God keep you from responding to Him in everything. Samuel was just a boy when God called him by name to be a prophet for the nation of Israel. (1 Sam. 3) Jeremiah also was a young man who expressed his fears of inadequacy but God knew better. (Jer. 1) The prophet Isaiah fell on his face as one dead when confronted with a vision of God in Heaven. He felt the immense separation of a holy God and sinful man. God sent an angel to cleanse him and prepare him for his mission from God. (Isa. 6)

God accepts us as we are and by His grace calls us to Himself. His presence is promised to those who seek Him wholeheartedly. Spiritual maturity is not measured by Sundays in the pew but by hours on the mountain.

5. *Begin the Ascent Even if You Don't Understand the Entire Process.*

The servants of the wedding feast didn't know why they were filling wine jugs with water. Abraham didn't know where he was going when God told him to pack up his family and possession and move. But he went.

When you don't let excuses keep us from the mountain top it releases the revelation of God upon your life. He rewards those who diligently seek Him and diligence is required when there are so many good reasons not to seek His face today.

God is looking for people who won't give excuses for why they can't pursue Him. Your excuses keep you at a distance from your Heavenly Father.

The same God who turned the water in to wine and changed the circumstances from bad to good is the same God that will meet you where you are and make a way where there seems to be none. When you press past the excuses to spend time in the presence of God it paves the way for the next step in the mountain journey; the invitation of God to Come See!

Come See!

and they saw the God of Israel; and under His feet there appeared to be a pavement of sapphire, as clear as the sky itself.

Exodus 24:10

that the God of our Lord Jesus Christ, the Father of glory, may give to you a spirit of wisdom and of revelation in the knowledge of Him.

Ephesians 1:17

"Blessed are the pure in heart, for they shall see God.

Matthew 5:8

And the Word became flesh, and dwelt among us, and we saw His glory, glory as of the only begotten from the Father, full of grace and truth.

John 1:14

*Six days later Jesus *took with Him Peter and James and John his brother, and *led them up on a high mountain by themselves. And He was transfigured before them; and His face shone like the sun, and His garments became as white as light.*

Matthew 17:1-2

6

Revelation

and they saw the God of Israel; and under His feet there appeared to be a pavement of sapphire, as clear as the sky itself.

Exodus 24:10

"**A**nd they saw God" Moses, Aaron, Joshua, Nadab and Abihu and the 70 elders of Israel saw God! He opened their spiritual eyes and allowed them to see into the supernatural world where God exists. They had responded to the call, made sacrifices, moved in obedience and now the revelation of God was their reward. Imagine how this experience shaped and strengthened their faith in Him? As you ascend the mountain, God will make Himself known to you too.

All We Know of God is What He Has Chosen to Reveal

Without the revelation of God, the Holy Spirit, illuminating your darkened and veiled mind to supernatural realities, you cannot know and experience who God is and His activity in your life and the world around you. Without God's proactive intervention and illumination by His Holy Spirit, you cannot understand, recognize nor comprehend His written Word, the Holy Bible, nor His spoken Word, His still inner voice. All we know of God is what He has chosen to reveal to us. No revelation, no relationship.

Obedience Releases Revelation

If you want the revelation of God in your life then you must first obey His commandments. Your obedience to the Word of God releases His revelation, His manifest presence, in your life. The revelation of God builds and strengthens your relationship to Him. God's revelation is primary to relationship and your obedience to Him unlocks His revelation. Obedience unlocks the door of revelation and revelation paves the path to relationship. Do not expect greater revelation and deeper intimacy with Christ if you are not first walking in obedience to His Word. If you are stuck in a rut in your relationship with God, ask the Holy Spirit to show you where you are not walking in obedience to His Word. The progression of obedience, revelation, and relationship is seen in Jesus' words in John 14:

> *He who has My commandments and keeps them is the one*
> *who loves Me; and he who loves Me will be loved by My*
> *Father, and I will love him and will disclose Myself to him.*
> *John 14:21*

Notice how obedience *"He who has my commandments and keeps them"* comes before revelation and relationship. The reward of obedience is God will *"disclose"* Himself to you. Disclose is just another word for reveal. Disclose

He will not reveal more of Himself until you are obeying what you already know—or has been revealed to you by Him.

means, "to make know, to make apparent, to manifest, to reveal." Through obedience God manifests His presence in your life.

God has given you access to His revelation through obedience to His commandments. He is willing, wanting and waiting to disclose, or reveal, Himself to you! You don't have to beg, bribe or beat yourself up hoping for more of God. He invites you into His presence and points you down the path of obedience.

How often do we pursue our own desires, lusts and agendas, living for ourselves, walking in disobedience and then wonder why we experience so little of God? Is it no wonder we have so little of God when we give Him so little of ourselves?

Jesus promised, *"I will not leave you as orphans; I will come to you".* *(Jn. 14:18)* He calls out to you "Come up!" on the mountain and "Come see!" Him, and He has promised not to leave you alone but to come to you as well!

God also desires to give you a "spirit of wisdom", (Eph. 1:17) or supernatural wisdom, so you may know Him in greater and greater manifestations. But He will not reveal more of Himself until you are obeying what you already know—or what has been previously revealed to you by Him:

> *that the God of our Lord Jesus Christ, the Father of glory, may give to you a spirit of wisdom and of revelation in the knowledge of Him.*
>
> *Ephesians 1:17*

Obedience is the key that unlocks greater manifestations and revelations of God in your life. But just as obedience unlocks revelation, disobedience locks the door and darkens your spiritual eyes and separates you from the knowledge of God:

> *"Blessed are the pure in heart, for they shall see God.*
>
> *Matthew 5:8*

Close Encounters of the God Kind

One of the most endearing qualities of God is he is very social-an extrovert if you will. You may be surprised that all throughout the Scriptures He looks for and makes opportunities to visit and interact with mankind on a very personal level. (See chapter 3) Theologians have a fancy word for these God-visits, "theophanies" (Greek: theos="God" + phaino= "appear").

But wait a minute! How can anyone see God when plainly in Scripture it says no man can see God and live? Moses made this clear by quoting the very words of God Himself when he asked Him to show His Glory:

> But He said, "You cannot see My face, for no man can see
> Me and live!"
>
> Exodus 33:20

The Apostle John, two-thousand years later in the New Testament, emphatically supports Moses' conclusions as well:

> No one has seen God at any time; the only begotten God
> who is in the bosom of the Father, He has explained Him.
>
> John 1:18

> No one has seen God at any time; if we love one another,
> God abides in us, and His love is perfected in us.
>
> 1 John 4:12

At first, one might think this is a major contradiction but a little clarification will clear this up and open to you a beautiful and deeper understanding of Jesus and His activity in the Old Testament. In a nutshell, the above Scriptures are correct, no one can see the full glory of God and live. His holiness and awesomeness is so powerful and beyond comprehension that any created thing cannot withstand the full revelation of His Glory and Being and live. The key word is "full" revelation. God is so transcendent and beyond anything created that He must limit His revelation of Himself to what man can comprehend and still survive. He descended on Mt. Sinai and covered the mountain in a thick cloud. That cloud wasn't just for visual effect, it also protected the people from exposure to a measure of His Glory they could not withstand and live. To say, "no man can see His face and live", is like saying no one can see God fully in all His Glory and live.

But what about those like Jacob and Moses, among others we will soon learn, who did see the face of God and live?

So Jacob named the place Peniel, for he said, "I have seen God face to face, yet my life has been preserved."

Genesis 32:30

Thus the LORD used to speak to Moses face to face, just as a man speaks to his friend.

Exodus 33:11a

How do we reconcile these seemingly apparent contradictions? Did the men of the Old Testament see the face of God or not? In a simple yet profound truth- these contradictions are reconciled in the person of Jesus Christ.

How do we reconcile these seemingly apparent contradictions? Did the men of the Old Testament see the face of God or not? In a simple yet profound truth- these contradictions are reconciled in the person of Jesus Christ. Jesus is God in the flesh. Jesus is God clothed in humanity and covered enough for man to receive this revelation of God and not die. When God came down in the cool of the day to talk with Adam and Eve that was Christ! When Jacob wrestled with God face to face he was wrestling with Christ! When Moses spoke to God face to face, just as a man speaks to his friend, he was talking to Christ! This was the pre-incarnate Christ, that is, Jesus before he was born physically of the virgin Mary. When you grasp this truth it will revolutionize your reading of the Old Testament. Jesus Christ is all through the Old Testament and you may have not even known it until now! Jesus our Savior was involved with redemption and the salvation of mankind from the very beginning—it did not start with his birth in a manger on a cold starry night in Bethlehem.

I hope I have whet your appetite for a seek-n-find Jesus in the Old

Testament because the theophany on top Mt. Sinai in Exodus twenty-four was not his first visit. Let's explore some of the theophanies, or God visitations, recorded in the Old Testament to build up our faith to prepare for our own encounters.

In the Garden

The desire and heart of God to be in relationship with mankind is seen from our very beginnings as recorded in the creation account in Genesis. Not only did He have an active part in the creation of the universe and our world but He literally had a hands-on approach to our existence:

> *Then the LORD God formed man of dust from the ground, and breathed into his nostrils the breath of life; and man became a living being.*
>
> *Genesis 2:7*

We were fashioned by His hands and then He breathed into us His Spirit and we became a living being. He deposited His Spirit within us, giving us a spirit, a supernatural part of us that allows us to connect, communicate and relate with a supernatural God. That is one of the primary

We were carefully and purposefully created with the supernatural capacity, our spirit, to interact with God. We were made in His image and His likeness for that very reason. You were created for relationship.

characteristics that separate mankind from the animal kingdom. We were carefully and purposefully created with the supernatural capacity, our spirit, to interact with God. We were made in His image and His likeness for that very reason. You were created for relationship:

> *God created man in His own image, in the image of God He created him; male and female He created them.*
>
> *Genesis 1:27*

Technically speaking then, Genesis 3 records the first theophany-where God visits man, before that is God creating man not visiting him. This visitation from God takes place just after Adam and Eve fell into temptation by the serpent and disobeyed God by eating of the forbidden fruit:

> *They heard the sound of the LORD God walking in the garden in the cool of the day, and the man and his wife hid themselves from the presence of the LORD God among the trees of the garden.*
>
> *Genesis 3:8*

From this first theophany, it seems likely and not far off to infer that God had a habit of making early morning visits to the garden to talk with Adam and Eve. The fact they heard Him walking in the garden tells us He was in physical form. Unfortunately this morning a drastic shift had occurred. Remember, obedience increases revelation and disobedience decreases it. This is a sad reminder of that reality.

What can we learn from this first visit from God? We have been created for relationship. God has given us a spirit, a supernatural capacity, to communicate and relate to God who is Supernatural. Just as God visited Adam and Eve on a regular basis so He desires fellowship with us on a regular basis. It is through God's revelation of Himself that we come to know Him. We cannot know God apart from His revelation by His Holy Spirit. Disobedience limits God's revelation in our lives but obedience is the channel that opens us up to greater revelation.

The Captain of the LORD'S host

Just before Joshua was to lead the Israelites into battle against the city of Jericho he was surveying the surrounding area and had the following encounter with a man with a drawn sword in Joshua 5:

Now it came about when Joshua was by Jericho, that he lifted up his eyes and looked, and behold, a man was standing opposite him with his sword drawn in his hand, and Joshua went to him and said to him, "Are you for us or for our adversaries?" He said, "No; rather I indeed come now as captain of the host of the LORD." And Joshua fell on his face to the earth, and bowed down, and said to him, "What has my lord to say to his servant?" The captain of the LORD'S host said to Joshua, "Remove your sandals from your feet, for the place where you are standing is holy." And Joshua did so.

Joshua 5:13-15

God appeared to Moses in the desert as a fire that did not consume the bush and gave him the same commandment:

Then He said, "Do not come near here; remove your sandals from your feet, for the place on which you are standing is holy ground."

Exodus 3:5

This man is much more than a human and even more than an angel. Only God can make holy and receive worship in this fashion. This clearly seems to imply that this was Jesus-and what a fitting title, "Captain of the Host of the LORD". In this encounter Jesus gave Joshua instructions on how to proceed in battle to conquer the inhabitants of the city of Jericho. Just as God appeared to Moses as a flaming bush and gave him his orders so now he appears to Joshua as a military commander and gives him his marching orders.

In your time of need for direction and guidance God is there for you too. Let him be your Captain, your commanding officer, submit to his authority and let him lead you into battle. Before any great or small endeavors seek His face for answers. Although your enemies may outnumber you, you are not alone, His sword is drawn, He is fighting for you.

The Angel of the LORD

Gideon was called to battle by an angel of the LORD in Judges 6:

> *The angel of the LORD appeared to him and said to him,*
> *"The LORD is with you, O valiant warrior."*
>
> *Judges 6:12*

Gideon's response to this visitation was to request proof this was the LORD. So he prepared an offering of food that the angel of God caused fire to spring up out of a rock and consume just before vanishing. Gideon's response to this visual display of the supernatural was as follows:

> *When Gideon saw that he was the angel of the LORD, he said, "Alas, O Lord GOD! For now I have seen the angel of the LORD face to face." The LORD said to him, "Peace to you, do not fear; you shall not die."*
>
> *Judges 6:22-23*

Gideon was given proof this was God. He knew the warning no one could see the face of God and live and he was afraid he was going to die. The LORD consoles (notice "angel" has been dropped) him and tells him he is not going to die. Here again we have a theophany, a visitation of Christ. This encounter brings up another key to seeing Christ in the Old Testament. Often in the Bible account when an angel of the LORD is mentioned it is the pre-incarnate Christ. How can you know when it is Christ and when it is an angel? When an angel of the LORD receives worship then it is Christ because only God is to be worshipped. Any messenger of God sent by God will not accept worship that belongs to God alone.

Before we transition into the New Testament I want to leave you with some other Old Testament Scripture references that very well may be pre-incarnate theophanies of Christ. These will make for you some wonderful mountain top Bible study moments.

Examples of other Old Testament Theophanies

Genesis 16:13; 17:1; 18:1-3; 32:24-30
Numbers 12:6-8
Judges 13:3-6,18
2 Kings 19:35
Zechariah 3:1-2

Let's now take a brief look at what the New Testament teaches us about God's revelation.

You've Got Jesus!

As a New Testament believer God has provided for you the supreme and ultimate revelation of himself in the person of Jesus Christ. The Apostle John beautifully articulates this reality in John 1:

> *And the Word became flesh, and dwelt among us, and we saw His glory, glory as of the only begotten from the Father, full of grace and truth.*
>
> *John 1:14*

The Apostle Paul understood the nature of Christ when he penned his letter to the church in Colossae:

> *He is the image of the invisible God,...*
>
> *Colossians 1:15a*

Jesus knew who He was and made it very clear on a number of occasions and here is just one example when He was teaching his disciples in John 14:

> *"Do you not believe that I am in the Father, and the Father is in Me? The words that I say to you I do not speak on My own initiative, but the Father abiding in Me does His works.*
>
> *John 14:10*

Ascending the Mountain of God

When asked by Christ who he thought Jesus was, the Apostle Peter responded boldly and declared he was the Son of the living God. That revelation came not by man but by God Himself:

> He *said to them, "But who do you say that I am?" Simon
> Peter answered, "You are the Christ, the Son of the living
> God." And Jesus said to him, "Blessed are you, Simon
> Barjona, because flesh and blood did not reveal this to you,
> but My Father who is in heaven.
>
> Matthew 16:15-17

God the Father through His Holy Spirit desires to reveal Himself to you through His Son, Jesus Christ. The key to walking and experiencing greater revelation is to pursue the person of Jesus. In Exodus twenty-four Jesus was waiting on top of that mountain for Moses to ascend into the Glory Cloud and right now Jesus is waiting for you on Mt. Zion.

Jesus Lets His Glory Shine

> Six days later Jesus *took with Him Peter and James and
> John his brother, and *led them up on a high mountain by
> themselves. And He was transfigured before them; and
> His face shone like the sun, and His garments became as
> white as light.
>
> Matthew 17:1-2

Here we have another mountain top experience that is strikingly similar to the Exodus twenty-four Mt. Sinai encounter. Tradition says this high mountain was likely Mt. Hermon located on the northern border of Israel with the town of Caesarea Philippi at its base. Caesarea Philippi is the place where Peter made his confession of Christ the Messiah in Matthew 16. It is a tall mountain, 9,200 ft above sea level, and whose three peaks are covered in snow most of year. It is no coincidence Jesus chose to transform Himself on top of a mountain.

83

Matthew seventeen begins by stating, "six days later". Later in Exodus 24:16 we will read that Moses waited six days before God called him up into the Glory Cloud. Jesus takes Peter, James, and John with him up on a high mountain and is transfigured before them. His transformation is described as *"his face shown like the sun and his garments became as white as light."* What a revelation of His Glory! For just a moment Jesus allowed a portion of His Glory, His Godness, to shine through His earthly garment of skin. During this brilliant display of light a cloud descends upon the mountain top, Moses and Elijah appear beside Him and the voice of speaks from the cloud and says, *"This is My dearly loved Son, who brings Me great joy. Listen to Him."* (Mat. 17:5) The disciples can only fall on their faces in fear of this overwhelming, terrifying and spectacular revelation of Jesus. Moses represents the Law, he was given the Ten Commandments and the Law. Elijah represents the prophets. The Old Testament is summed up and referred to as a whole as the Law and Prophets. When the disciples get up from the ground it says:

> And when they looked up, Moses and Elijah were gone, and they saw only Jesus.
>
> Matthew 17:8

When they looked up, they saw only Jesus. Jesus came as a fulfillment of the Law and Prophets. The Law drove man to admit he needed a savior, the Prophets pointed man to the savior, the Messiah, Jesus Christ. Moses and Elijah were gone because now Jesus opened the way to a New Covenant, not a covenant of law and judgment but one of grace and mercy:

> For the Law was given through Moses; grace and truth were realized through Jesus Christ.
>
> John 1:17

When we meet Christ on the mountain of Zion He brings mercy

and grace. We may fall on our faces in response to His Glory and awesomeness revealed to us but when it's over He does what He did on Mt. Hermon:

> *Then Jesus came over and touched them. "Get up," He said.*
> *"Don't be afraid."*
>
> *Matthew 17:7*

In our mountain top experience with the Risen Savior He too brings comfort as His presence envelopes us, touches us and gently says, "Get up. Don't be afraid." Mt. Sinai brought the law and in its wake fell judgment, fear and trembling but from Mt. Zion rings the Gospel, the Good News of redemption, and to all who hear receive grace, mercy and love.

You Need Revelation

Revelation is a supernatural experience where God allows a person to see, experience or know what was previously hidden and unattainable without God's proactive intervention. The ultimate goal of Divine revelation is to shed light on the nature, character, person and works of God as revealed through His Son Jesus Christ.

We need the revelation of God for salvation but that is just the beginning. Through God's revelation He shows us Himself. But we also need His revelation so we can understand ourselves, our children, our marriage, our jobs, our place in this world, our mission from God, our hang-ups, our gifts and talents, our strengths as well as weaknesses-basically to show us how to navigate and live a godly and victorious life in this ungodly and fallen world.

Mt. Sinai brought the law and in its wake fell judgment, fear and trembling but from Mt. Zion rings the Gospel, the Good News of redemption, and to all who hear receive grace, mercy and love.

The Goals of Revelation: Identity and Relationship

Ultimately, I believe the supreme goal of God's revelation to you can be distilled into two areas: first, who you are in Christ and secondly, who Christ is in you. The first focuses on your identity, what Christ says you are and who you are in Him, and the latter focuses on your relationship, who Christ is in you and your relationship to Him. Revelation of your identity in Christ increases your understanding of yourself and who you really are. The revelation of who Christ is, His nature and character, puts you in greater intimacy and fellowship with God and enhances your relationship with Him.

Your True Identity: Who You Are In Christ

Greater revelations of who you are in Him and who He is in you draws you higher up the mountain and into His presence. It's not enough to know Christ but be unaware of who you are. A person who takes the time to know Christ but neglects the Holy Spirit's revelations of who he is and who God says he is will always live beneath his God given purpose and calling because his concept of who he is based on a worldly, personal, fragmented and darkened perspective and not on a heavenly, Christ-centered, supernatural, and enlightened perspective.

According to our self perceptions we will either live down to ungodly and inferior expectations or live up to godly and superior expectations.

Everyone lives and acts according to how they see themselves. Proverbs says it this way: "For as he thinks within himself, so he is." (Prov. 23:7) What you think you are determines what you do. Your self identity determines your outlook and actions in life. Thoughts precede actions. According to our self perceptions we will either live down to ungodly and inferior expectations or live up to godly and superior expectations. For example, if you see yourself from a world-centered identity that bombards you with lies telling you that you are worthless, ugly, needy, deficient, undeserving, failures and incapable then you will act accordingly. But if you know who you are in Christ; and your identity is shaped by who God says you are in the Word of God, then you will think and believe that in Christ you are complete, not lacking in anything. (Col. 2:10) You will believe what the Word says about you: That you are holy and without blame (Eph. 1:4; 1 Pet 1:16), that you have peace that is beyond comprehension (Phil. 4:7),

There are many believers, those in Christ, who still have not broken off their world-centered identity and as a result are not living the abundant life full of victory. It's not enough to know Christ but you must know who you are in Christ.

you are forgiven and washed in the Blood (Eph. 1:7), you are healed (Isa. 53:5), and you are greatly loved. (Rom. 1:7; Eph. 2:4) Someone who knows who they are in Christ will respond and live according to their Christ given identity. There are many believers who still have not broken off their world-centered identity and as a result are not living the abundant life full of victory. They are living down to their false identity in the world rather than living up to their identity in Christ. It is not enough to know Christ but you must equally know who you are in Christ.

But a revelation of Christ in you is incomplete without the fullness, or other half to the truth of that revelation, that you are in Christ:

The greatest revelations you will receive from God on the mountain top speak to your identity in Him and His identity in you. In His presence He begins to lovingly show you who we really are and how He has wonderfully created you. He accepts you as you are, broken, hurt, jaded, fearful, distrustful and a shadow of who you are meant to be, but loves you enough to not leave you in your pitiful condition. He brings healing to the wounds and areas of your life that have been ravaged by the darkness of this world and as only our Creator has the right and knowledge to do He shows you who He really created you to be. The more you get to know Him, the safer you feel in His presence, the more you trust Him with your hurts and secrets, the more He is able to lovingly and gently dismantle the false identities you have believed and rebuild you in His image.

The Foundation of Your Relationship: Who Christ is In You

It is a mighty revelation to know Christ is in you. He is in you to empower and guide and carry you through every valley and to the peak of His mountain. But a revelation of Christ in you is incomplete without the fullness, or other half to the truth of that revelation, that you are in Christ:

> In that day you will know that I am in My Father, and you in Me, and I in you.
>
> John 14:20

Many grasp the profound truth of Christ coming into their life at the moment of salvation. We are taught to repeat the sinner's prayer and ask Jesus to forgive our sins and come into our heart. Thank God for the miracle of the new birth and the desire of our Savior to come make His abode, His dwelling place, within us! But many do not take the next step.

You asked Jesus to come into your heart, now Jesus is asking you to come into His heart.

They have not been taught that asking Jesus into your life is only half of the miracle. Now that Jesus has given Himself to you to live in you, you must now give yourself to Him so you may live in Him. It's almost strange, but think of it this way: You asked Jesus to come into your heart, now Jesus is asking you to come into His heart.

And so God brings us to the foot of Mt. Zion in the instant we surrender our life to Him and ask Him to come into our heart and life to rule and to reign. In salvation, He transports us from the bondage of sin, the land of slavery, our personal Egypt we were sentenced and hopelessly condemned to by our sins and he exchanges our chains and filthy rags for hiking boots and white robes of righteousness. Now at the foot of the mountain we must pursue the higher revelation and lay hold of Christ for which He has laid hold of us—the supernatural reality that not only is He in us but that we are in Him. And in the midst of revelation we will step up and in to the next leg of our mountain experience and hear His call to Come Feast!

Come Feast!

Yet He did not stretch out His hand against the nobles of the sons of Israel; and they saw God, and they ate and drank.

Exodus 24:11

"I am the living bread that came down out of heaven; if anyone eats of this bread, he will live forever; and the bread also which I will give for the life of the world is My flesh."

John 6:51

"For My flesh is true food, and My blood is true drink. "He who eats My flesh and drinks My blood abides in Me, and I in him. "As the living Father sent Me, and I live because of the Father, so he who eats Me, he also will live because of Me. "This is the bread which came down out of heaven; not as the fathers ate and died; he who eats this bread will live forever."

John 6:55-58

And when He had taken some bread and given thanks, He broke it and gave it to them, saying, "This is My body which is given for you; do this in remembrance of Me." And in the same way He took the cup after they had eaten, saying, "This cup which is poured out for you is the new covenant in My blood.

Luke 22:19-20

7

Fellowship

and they saw God, and they ate and drank.

Exodus 24:11

I was enjoying a potluck meal after service sitting at a table surrounded by friends when the unthinkable happened. I had my plate full of a variety of interesting homemade casseroles and side dishes and was going around the plate one bite at a time savoring the experience when it happened. I raised my fork to my mouth and was expecting a savory cut of breaded sirloin but instead got a mouthful of liver. I hate liver. My mouth had been violated. I wanted to spit it out but what kind of manners is that? And besides, someone at my table probably was the one who had brought the dish. I didn't want to hurt anyone's feelings so I chewed, and chewed and focused all my will and grown up tolerance on getting it down quickly and uneventfully. When you experience the sustaining and nourishing presence of God you don't have to worry about God surprising you with liver!

O taste and see that the LORD is good;

Psalms 34:8a

Spending time in the presence of God nourishes your spiritual man. When you neglect the presence of God by avoiding the mountain of Zion, it takes its toll on you spiritually. You will become weak and vulnerable to temptation and worldly desires. Jesus understood the power and preeminence of spiritual nourishment when He was asked by the disciples to eat:

> Jesus *said to them, "My food is to do the will of Him who sent Me and to accomplish His work.
>
> John 4:34

There is sustaining power and supernatural energy received while basking in the presence of God. When you feel weak run to the mountain; God has prepared a spiritual meal waiting for you when you arrive.

Jesus is Recruiting Climbers not Campers

Have you ever heard of a sermon so demanding the crowd complained it was too hard and in the middle of the message began to get up and walk out? Or a sermon so offensive the next Sunday only half the people return? I'm not talking about bad, uninteresting preaching either. I'm talking about a message so strong and demanding it scatters most of the flock. A sermon preached from the pulpit to deliberately and unequivocal offend the listeners, and afterwards, when most have already walked out of the sanctuary, the preacher turns to the choir behind him and asks, "You going to walk out too?" Jesus preached such a sermon in John 6.

At the beginning of the chapter Jesus had supernaturally multiplied five small loaves of bread to feed over 5,000 people with twelve large baskets of bread leftover! As a result of this amazing demonstration of power and ability to effortlessly feed the hungry, Jesus perceived the people intended to forcefully make Him their King! Jesus' time was not ready, nor was His Heavenly purpose to be their earthly king, so He escaped to the mountain side. The next day the crowd found Him in the synagogue in Capernaum. They were again hoping for a miracle, and a meal, from their would-be king, so He took the opportunity to teach. As a result of His miracles, Jesus had attracted a very large crowd of people. Now it was time for Him to find out who meant business and who was just along for the ride.

Take the time to read John 6 and specifically verses 23-61 and notice how persistent and belligerently offensive His message was to them. In verse 41 they began to openly grumble about His claims to be the bread of life:

> *Therefore the Jews were grumbling about Him, because He said, "I am the bread that came down out of heaven."*
> *John 6:41*

Now you might think it would be a good time for Jesus to explain Himself, but He doesn't. Instead, He repeats Himself again:

> *"Truly, truly, I say to you, he who believes has eternal life. 48 "I am the bread of life. 49 "Your fathers ate the manna in the wilderness, and they died. 50 "This is the bread which comes down out of heaven, so that one may eat of it and not die. 51 "I am the living bread that came down out of heaven; if anyone eats of this bread, he will live forever; and the bread also which I will give for the life of the world is My flesh."*
> *John 6:47-51*

Jesus was making sure they heard Him right, and that they knew they heard Him right. But because they were stuck in the natural, and they were offended by His words, they missed what He meant. And that's how Jesus separated His disciples from the followers.

He knew they were offended. He knew they knew misunderstanding His message and that's EXACTLY what He wanted! To be offensive!

Even when they started arguing among themselves as to what He meant, He didn't attempt to clarify but rather continued to repeat Himself, but now in grossly graphic detail: Count the number of times in the following passage Jesus talks about eating His flesh and drinking His blood:

> *52 Then the Jews began to argue with one another, saying, "How can this man give us His flesh to eat?" 53 So Jesus said to them, "Truly, truly, I say to you, unless you eat the flesh of the Son of Man and drink His blood, you have no life in yourselves. 54 "He who eats My flesh and drinks My blood has eternal life, and I will raise him up on the last day. 55 "For My flesh is true food, and My blood is true drink. 56 "He who eats My flesh and drinks My blood abides in Me, and I in him. 57 "As the living Father sent Me, and I live because of the Father, so he who eats Me, he also will live because of Me. 58 "This is the bread which came down out of heaven; not as the fathers ate and died; he who eats this bread will live forever."*
>
> *John 6:52-58*

Jesus never intended on drawing a crowd to win a popularity contest. He preached His message to separate who meant business from those who were along for the thrill. He was recruiting climbers not campers. He didn't have time for those who wanted only to be amazed by His miracles, or awed by the power and authority by which He spoke, or entertained by His parables. His time was too precious and His purpose too important. His mission was to draw all men unto Himself so that they might enjoy God with a front row seat, not from the back pew where they could slip out unnoticed after they had done God a favor.

Jesus never intended on drawing a crowd to win a popularity contest. He preached His message to separate who meant business from those who were along for the thrill.

God is asking you to "partake" of Him. He wants you to feed long after you have tasted salvation. He is calling you to leave the valley behind. Salvation is just the appetizers, there is so much more in the banquet of God to enjoy! Don't settle for crackers and cheese when steak and lobster are waiting! But sadly, many believers do settle. They snack here and there on God and get just enough of Him to get by until next Sunday's feeding. They never fully engage in God and then continually wonder why their spiritual life lacks fulfillment and purpose.

Two Types of Followers

There were two types of followers of Jesus found in John 6. There were those who followed from a distance and when commitment was required responded:

> From this time many of His disciples went back into the things behind, and walked no more with Him.
>
> John 6:66

They were what I call Campers, Followers of Convenience. Then there were the Twelve who responded:

> Then Jesus said to the Twelve, Do you also wish to go away? Then Simon Peter answered Him, Lord, to whom shall we go? You have the Words of eternal life. And we have believed and have known that You are the Christ, the Son of the living God.
>
> John 6:67-69

They were what I call Followers of Necessity, or Climbers.

Which type of follower are you? Are you a camper or a climber? Are you a follower of convenience or follower of necessity? Are you a back seat or front row believer? Are you following from the fringe or pressing through the crowd. Are you a friend of God or distant relative? It's time you move on from believing and start feeding. God wants you on the mountain seven days a week, not just on the "Lord's Day."

How Do Increase Your Hunger for God?

The following are four ways to increase your hunger to pursue God up the mountain.

1.   Ask for a Hunger to Know God

I know a steady diet of Krispy Kreme Donuts for breakfast and Papa John's Pizza for dinner will cause me to grow out of my pants and feel lethargic and tired. But that doesn't always keep me from indulging myself in those unhealthy foods. They are tasty, cheap and very convenient. My defense for overcoming those unhealthy foods is to ask God to remove my appetite for them and replace it with a desire for healthy foods. It is no different in spiritual matters. It's not enough to know you need to eat healthy; you got to want it. And want it badly. It's not enough to know you need God, and more of Him. You're desire for God must overwhelm every other desire in your life. Read the heart's desires penned in the following psalms:

> My soul longeth, yea, even fainteth for the courts of the LORD: my heart and my flesh crieth out for the living God.
>
> Psalm 84:2

> For a day in thy courts [is] better than a thousand. I had rather be a doorkeeper in the house of my God, than to dwell in the tents of wickedness.
>
> Psalm 84:10

> My soul is crushed with longing After Your ordinances at all times.
>
> Psalms 119:20

> I opened my mouth wide and panted, For I longed for Your commandments.
>
> Psalms 119:131

Seven times each day I stop and shout praises for the way you keep everything running right.

Psalm 119:164

Stretched out my hands to you, as thirsty for you as a desert thirsty for rain.

Psalm 143:6

Praise ye the LORD. Praise the LORD, O my soul. While I live will I praise the LORD: I will sing praises unto my God while I have any being.

Psalm 146:1-2

Increasing Desire Through the Psalms

Reading, meditating, and praying the Psalms back to God is one of the surest ways to increase your hunger for God. Ask God to give you the passion for Him that is poured out into the Psalms. May your heart cry be the same of Moses who asked of God, *"And he said, I beseech You, let me see Your glory." (Ex. 33:18)*

Your hunger for God will increase and be satisfied, the Bible declares it:

Blessed [are] they which do hunger and thirst after righteousness: for they shall be filled.

Matthew 5:6

You must seek out and surround yourself with men and women of God who when pricked ooze holiness, righteousness, and zeal for God.

2. *Seek Out and Spend Time With People Who are Hungry for God*

Be not deceived: Evil companionships corrupt good morals.

1 Corinthians 15:33

The Principle of Influential Proximation

It's a fact, your mother knew what she was doing when she wanted to see who your friends were before she let you go out with them. She knew that bad company corrupts good character. But we don't have to be as extreme to see what I like to call, the Principle of Influential Proximation, at work. The Principle of Influential Proximation states, the longer and closer in relationship you are to a person, or group, the more like them you will become. To apply this principle to your advantage, you must seek out and surround yourself with men and women of God who when pricked ooze holiness, righteousness, and zeal for God.

The Example of Jesus as a Boy

At 12 years old Jesus was aware of this principle when his family went to Jerusalem for the Feast of the Passover. After three days of searching for their son they found him in the Temple Courts:

> *in the Temple Courts, sitting among the teachers, listening to them and asking them questions. Everyone who heard him was amazed at his understanding and his answers.*
> *Luke 2:46-47*

Evidently, Jesus at a young age didn't have the opportunity to surround himself with learned godly men and He wasn't leaving until He got His fill! Who have you sought out to listen to and ask questions as Jesus did? Who have you surrounded yourself with whose walk is worthy of the call?

The Example of the Apostle Paul

The Apostle Paul also understood this principle and encouraged the recipients of his letter to the church in Corinth: *"Be ye followers of me, even as I also [am] of Christ." (1 Cor. 11:1)* So I exhort you to seek out a spiritual guide. Don't let that phrase scare you just because the

New Age movement has adopted it. You need more than a once a week dose from someone behind a pulpit to become more like Christ. If the only time you see your pastor is at church then that doesn't qualify. Ask God to bring into your life a mentor to whom you can walk along side and watch how they live. Someone who also sees how you live and you give permission for them to speak into your life through encouragement, exhortation, and even rebuke when needed.

3. Be a Person of One Book

And when he puts forth his own sheep, he goes before them, and the sheep follow him. For they know his voice. And they will not follow a stranger, but will flee from him, for they do not know the voice of strangers.

John 10:4-5

In the beginning was the Word, and the Word was with God, and the Word was God.

John 1:1

To know God is to know His voice and to know His voice is to know His Word.

I had the privilege in my younger years in ministry to serve as an Associate Pastor for a small congregation whose pastor was nearing retirement. He had served the church faithfully for over 20 years and was a man of impeccable integrity and a student of God's Word. Young as I was though, there was one thing that disappointed me about him; his library. He had very few books. I was convinced a pastor in the ministry as long as him should have shelves and shelves of books lining his entire office. My budding collection was growing and already tripled his.

I asked him about it one day. He told me as a young man the Holy Spirit told him to "Beware of man's writings." So from that point on he became a person of one Book, the Bible. His most important books to him were his Strong's concordance, a Greek New Testament, a

Hebrew Old Testament, and some Greek and Hebrew grammars. He had no formal education beyond high school but he would read the New Testament from the Greek and even taught a Greek class for interested Bible students. I respected his thoughts and insights on Scripture more than other pastors I knew with Bible and Theology degrees. He was truly a Holy Spirit taught man of the Word. His revelations were from the Holy Spirit not Matthew Henry.

4. *Wait for the Holy Spirit to Show you God*

As spiritual and theologically sound as they may be, be careful not to get caught up in the latest popular authors and spiritual public figures. Don't let them rob you of God speaking directly into your life by watching, listening, or reading them more than you are spending time in God's Word. I am not saying don't feed upon the anointed messages from godly men and women God has placed in your life, but pay attention to how much you are spending with

Make the time to hear, read, study, memorize, meditate, confess and apply the whole Holy Bible, both the Old and New Testaments in your search for intimacy.

them. I've known people who watch or listen to three or four sermons a day from various ministers of the Gospel, literally logging in dozens of hours a week, but rarely cracked their Bible open for themselves. They could quote their favorite sound bites and spiritual maxims from the last sermons they heard, but in reality, they were living a vicarious Christian life through experiences of others that had been on the mountain. They had no original words from the Lord for themselves.

> *that the God of our Lord Jesus Christ, the Father of glory,*
> *may give to you a spirit of wisdom and of revelation in the*
> *knowledge of Him.*
> *Ephesians 1:17*

I have been inspired many times by reading the experiences and thoughts of great, godly spiritual authors of the past and present but during this season of my life God is directing me to lay aside those second hand experiences and allow the Holy Spirit to show me directly what it means to know God! Refuse to settle for a vicarious relationship when you can experience the depth of God for yourself! Choose to saturate yourself in the Word of God. Make the time to hear, read, study, memorize, meditate, confess and apply the whole Holy Bible, both the Old and New Testaments, in your search for intimacy:

> *I have chosen a life of faithfulness. I have set your regulations in front of me. I have clung tightly to your written instructions. O LORD, do not let me be put to shame.*
>
> *Psalm 119:30-31*

Nothing can be more exciting than an intense spiritual encounter with God on the mountain. I long for those times when He manifests His glory in my life and pours out on me and in me refreshing waves of His presence, power and goodness.

There is a standing invitation from God to ascend the heavens and enter His Throne, and at times it seems the mountain opens up before us, and we are effortlessly ushered to the top. But most times we must be diligent and wait patiently as He prepares us for His presence. It is in those times He calls us to wait and how we wait determines our reward. Let's go to the next station on the mountain and answer the call to Come Wait!

Come Wait!

Now the LORD said to Moses, "Come up to Me on the mountain and remain there,"

Exodus 24:12a

The glory of the LORD rested on Mount Sinai, and the cloud covered it for six days; and on the seventh day He called to Moses from the midst of the cloud.

Exodus 24:16

"For Your salvation I wait, O LORD.

Genesis 49:18

Yet those who wait for the LORD Will gain new strength; They will mount up with wings like eagles, They will run and not get tired, They will walk and not become weary.

Isaiah 40:31

The LORD is good to those who wait for Him, To the person who seeks Him.

Lamentations 3:25

8

Determination

Moses, Aaron and his sons and the seventy elders of Israel had just finished partaking of a meal with God when God again called Moses to come up higher on the mountain to be with Him. God had manifested Himself spectacularly to the group of men but now it was time for Moses to leave the pack behind:

> *Now the LORD said to Moses, "Come up to Me on the mountain and remain there,"*
>
> *Exodus 24:12a*

With this invite God adds, *"and remain there,"* In other words, "Come up a little higher and wait." Moses obeys and sets his affairs in order (verse 14) and delegates his duties to Aaron and Hur and leaves with Joshua, his assistant, to climb higher up the mountain. And wait Moses does. In verse sixteen we learn how long:

> *The glory of the LORD rested on Mount Sinai, and the cloud covered it for six days; and on the seventh day He called to Moses from the midst of the cloud.*
>
> *Exodus 24:16*

Moses waited six whole days before God called to him from the Glory Cloud on the seventh day. Six days! Now why did God make Moses wait so long when he was so close to the top? To answer that question we must step back and see what God has taught us about waiting.

Waiting on the Lord

I did a Bible word search of the word "wait" and it brought up a number of relevant verses. I selected a few I thought were most helpful to this study. Take some time to meditate on the following Scriptures that teach us something about waiting on God. Even better, I encourage you to look up and read these Scriptures in your own Bible:

Scriptures On Waiting on the Lord

Lead me in Your truth and teach me, For You are the God of my salvation; For You I wait all the day.
Psalms 25:5

Wait for the LORD; Be strong and let your heart take courage; Yes, wait for the LORD.
Psalms 27:14

Rest in the LORD and wait patiently for Him;
Psalms 37:7a

My soul, wait in silence for God only, For my hope is from Him.
Psalms 62:5

You are my hiding place and my shield; I wait for Your word.
Psalms 119:114

I wait for the LORD, my soul does wait, And in His word do I hope.
Psalms 130:5

My soul waits for the Lord More than the watchmen for the morning; Indeed, more than the watchmen for the morning.

Psalms 130:6

Those who hopefully wait for Me will not be put to shame.

Isaiah 49:23b

Therefore, return to your God, Observe kindness and justice, And wait for your God continually.

Hosea 12:6

But as for me, I will watch expectantly for the LORD; I will wait for the God of my salvation. My God will hear me.

Micah 7:7

For our citizenship is in heaven, from which also we eagerly wait for a Savior, the Lord Jesus Christ;

Philippians 3:20

God has a lot to tell us about waiting on Him. According to the above Scriptures the Lord has given us at least eight examples on how He would have us wait for Him on the mountain.

How to Wait on the Lord

1. We are to wait continually. *(Ps. 25;5; Hos. 12:6)*
2. We are to wait courageously. *(Ps. 27:14)*
3. We are to wait patiently. *(Ps. 37:7)*
4. We are to wait silently. *(Ps. 62:5)*
5. We are to wait listening. *(Ps. 119:114)*
6. We are to wait expectantly. *(Ps. 130:6; Micah 7:7)*
7. We are to wait hopefully. *(Ps.130:5; Isa. 49:23)*
8. We are to wait eagerly. *(Phil. 3:20)*

Waiting on the Lord is a much more profound-and I dare say

challenging endeavor than at first perceived. No wonder many do not glean the benefits of waiting on the Lord because too often we are doing it all wrong. Based on the eight examples we have learned about waiting on the Lord, I have synthesized a working definition of the Biblical concept of waiting on the Lord.

Waiting on the Lord Defined

To wait on the Lord is deliberately pausing your soul-- to focus your thoughts, body and emotions and to be fully engaged in the moment, the present, the now; and listening in eager and hopeful expectation patiently and courageously anticipating, desiring and believing for God to reveal Himself to you.

Now that's sure a mouthful! Definitions are supposed to make things more clear. There are a lot of components to this definition but if I break it down a bit I think it will serve you well.

In the definition the phrase "pausing your soul" was likely a new concept for you. I based this phrase and word choice on the following two Scriptures that we studied that used the word soul: Psalm 62:5 and Psalm 130:5 (see above). Psalm 62:5 simply said *"My soul, wait in silence for God only"*. The psalmist who penned these words was speaking to himself and referring to his soul. Undoubtedly he was reminding himself to wait on God only, not on any other person, situation or savior. In the silence his mind likely had many competing voices pulling him towards fear and despair but "No soul! Even in the silence my hope comes from Him!"

Psalm 130:5 gives us more insight to the idea of pausing the soul:

> *I wait for the LORD, my soul does wait, And in His word do I hope.*
>
> Psalms 130:5

Here we have the focusing of the mind, will and emotions. The first "I" represents the body. The "soul" represents his mind. And he places his "hope" his emotions in His word. Based on these two passages of

Scripture to pause the soul means to deliberately focus your thoughts, body and emotions on God.

Now let's look at the next component of the definition, "and be fully engaged in the moment, the present, the now;". One of the biggest obstacles to pausing the soul is the challenge of being in the present. In other words, not to randomly think about past or future events as we wait on the Lord. God revealed himself to Moses as "I AM". (Ex.3:14) He is the Ever Present One. The better we can calm our souls and be with God in the moment, the now, the greater revelation becomes possible. We must continually fight to remain in the present. It is so easy to wander our thoughts into what we did earlier, yesterday, last week or what we're going to do later, tomorrow, next week. There are times God will lead us into our past or future to reveal Truth to us but usually if we are waiting on God and not in the present we are waiting distractedly.

The rest of the definition should flow smoothly if you take it slow. It's answering more of the how than the what. How should we wait? "listening in eager and hopeful expectation patiently and

> *There are times God will lead us into our past or future to reveal Truth to us but usually if we are waiting on God and not in the present we are waiting distractedly.*

courageously anticipating, desiring and believing for God to reveal Himself to you." This latter part of the definition was my best attempt at weaving all the descriptive verbs we learned from the eight ways God has shown us how to wait on Him.

Now you can read through the definition a few more times as well as meditate on the Scriptures and start the process of evaluating your effectiveness at waiting on the Lord and making improvements and adjustments as required.

We've come a long way in describing the "how" of waiting but have not addressed our initial question of why did God make Moses wait six days? I guess the simplest answer would be, "Because He's God!" and that would be correct but there are other Scriptures and examples in the Bible of waiting on the Lord and some of these give us benefits to waiting. It is because of the benefits of waiting on the Lord that we will come to a better understanding of why God waited so long to call Moses up the mountain. There are two benefits I want to mention specifically in the following two Scriptures:

Yet those who wait for the LORD Will gain new strength;
They will mount up with wings like eagles, They will run
and not get tired, They will walk and not become weary.

Isaiah 40:31

The LORD is good to those who wait for Him, To the person
who seeks Him.

Lamentations 3:25

Two major benefits of waiting on the Lord is you will receive supernatural strength and God will be good to you. Now that's two amazing reasons and motivations to wait on the Lord. In the specific case of Moses it's pretty certain God had him wait because he needed rest after the whirlwind of recent ordeals he had experienced since his burning bush encounter. I will develop the benefit and blessing of rest on the mountain more fully in chapter ten but for now I want to address another reason God often has us wait—it shows Him who is dedicated.

> *We want what we want like we want a drive through order at McDonald's: quick, cheap and easy. And this impatience and need for instant gratification barges in on our quiet times like a bull in a china shop.*

McDonald Christians

Unfortunately waiting is not something many like to do or are good at doing. We have been conditioned through microwaves, technology, fast food restaurants and the internet to have instant access to just about everything. Let's be honest, most of us are still about as impatient as a three year old toddler-we just are better at masking our tantrums-usually. We want what we want like we want a drive through order at McDonald's: quick, cheap and easy. And this impatience and need for instant gratification barges in on our quiet times like a bull in a china shop. Waiting on God and in His presence is definitely an act of determination and discipline and it proves to ourselves and to God just how serious we are. Don't be discouraged when it seems God is afar off and your prayers are falling short of his ears.

When you always mix haste and multi-tasking to your time with God it will inevitably dilute the power, impact and quality of your experience. That doesn't mean we should never squeeze a quick devotional in before heading off to work or pray in the car, or listen to the Bible on our IPod while we clean the kitchen, we should always look for ways to pursue Christ and include Him in our everyday activities but there is no substitute for yielding our total self, our mind, will and emotions and making time to wait--giving him our undivided and unrushed attention.

When we wait on the Lord as He has taught us to it releases His presence, power and goodness upon our life. The kind of waiting the Lord desires of us, the kind that releases His power and goodness is not like waiting in line at a grocery store but is waiting that requires discipline. It is waiting that involves persistence, courage, patience, silence, listening, expectancy and hope. It is not a waiting that means so much to slow down but more to actively remove distractions and gather our focus on God. As we wait it shows God our determination and prepares us for greater intimacy and revelation. When we are ready we now can answer the call to Come Learn!

Come Learn!

Now the LORD said to Moses, "Come up to Me on the mountain and remain there, and I will give you the stone tablets with the law and the commandment which I have written for their instruction."

Exodus 24:12

"It is He who reveals the profound and hidden things; He knows what is in the darkness, And the light dwells with Him.

Daniel 2:22

For the LORD gives wisdom; From His mouth come knowledge and understanding.

Proverbs 2:6

Behold, You desire truth in the innermost being, And in the hidden part You will make me know wisdom.

Psalms 51:6

that is, Christ Himself, (3) in whom are hidden all the treasures of wisdom and knowledge.

Colossians 2:2b,3

9

Instruction

Now the LORD said to Moses, "Come up to Me on the mountain and remain there, and I will give you the stone tablets with the law and the commandment which I have written for their instruction."

Exodus 24:12

We live in a technologically advanced age. Information has gone from only accessible at the local library to anyone with a smart phone can ask any question on any topic and in a microsecond receive an endless list of possible answers. We have now come to a place in human history where we are inundated with an endless barrage of information, facts, figures, blogs, websites, news media outlets, bestselling Self Help books, YouTube videos...And yet many still wander through life in a dim haze unsure of their purpose in life. We fill our days up existing paycheck to paycheck, Netflicks series episode to episode, Facebook alert to Instagram notice and never quite grasp true meaning and fulfilment out of life. Life is hard and at the end of the day we are left feeling empty with self-worth, confidence and satisfaction always temporary experiences that fade into the fog of reality all too quickly.

Many are hungry for answers and sit down at the table of worldly wisdom and before them is a menu with thousands of pages and millions of items. It is overwhelming and we are paralyzed and unable to decide what we would like the most. We scan the restaurant and see someone with an appealing plate and in an act of desperation cry out, "I'll have what their having." But we are left uncertain, wondering if our selection was the best one and fearful we overlooked something far better, or even worse, we won't like what we've got coming.

All is not hopeless. God has given us His Holy Spirit to guide us into all Truth:

> *"But when He, the Spirit of truth, comes, He will guide you*
> *into all the truth;*
>
> John 16:13

He has uniquely fashioned you and knows your every thought, ambition and innermost desire. He can guide you through the overwhelming menu of life and His recommendations and counsel can be trusted. One of the many priceless treasures of spending time with God on the mountain is He dispenses His wisdom freely without showing favoritism. James says it this way:

> *But if any of you lacks wisdom, let him ask of God, who*
> *gives to all generously and without reproach, and it will be*
> *given to him.*
>
> James 1:5

Let's ascend higher with Moses up Mt. Sinai and discover the instruction He received from God and then see what awaits us on Mt. Zion:

> *Now the LORD said to Moses, "Come up to Me on the*
> *mountain and remain there, and I will give you the stone*

*tablets with the law and the commandment which I have
written for their instruction."*

Exodus 24:12

On the mountain top in the Glory Cloud, Moses received from God all the instruction he needed to fulfill his purpose for God: the 10 Commandments, the Law (Sacrificial system, dietary, health and ceremonial laws), and instructions for building the Tabernacle. You too will find the answers to your problems and the supernatural wisdom to live the life God has intended you to live in His presence on the mountain top.

The Psalmist knew the reality and secret of wisdom:

*Behold, You desire truth in the innermost being, And in the
hidden part You will make me know wisdom.*

Psalms 51:6

Early morning mountain climbing, of Mt. Zion that is, requires discipline and self-sacrifice. There has been many a time, too many to count, when I paid the price, crucified the flesh, by the grace of God willed myself out of an early morning bed and devoted the early hours to prayer and Bible devotion and God dropped a supernatural word and instruction into my heart that afterwards I cried out to God, "Thank you Lord! That was exactly the insight and wisdom I needed!" It was a supernatural word from God, that had I not received the revelation from God it would have severely limited my ability and influence in a particular area of my life. Many times the wisdom and revelation from God is so profound to me I fear the outcome, the lack of that instruction in my life, had I not pressed in and sought the Lord in prayer. These moments of instruction are not received every mountain top encounter but their frequency motivate me back into His presence. When I miss those times I often wonder what great revelation I may have missed due to my laziness and spiritual lethargy.

Beware of Worldly Wisdom

What often keeps us from seeking wisdom from God is we look for and rely too heavily on wisdom from the world:

There is a way which seems right to a man, But its end is the way of death.

Proverbs 14:12

We must never forget the so called wisdom of this world is often misleading and we are fools to follow it before first seeking answers from God. The Apostle Paul warned the believers in Corinth of this reality in 1 Corinthians 3:

For the wisdom of this world is foolishness before God. For it is written, "He is THE ONE WHO CATCHES THE WISE IN THEIR CRAFTINESS";

1 Corinthians 3:19

The seduction to draw from our own understanding and to pursue wisdom from natural means is a powerful temptation and at its root an issue of pride and self-autonomy, or to be our own god. This desire for wisdom and power even outside of or in disobedience to the will of God was the first temptation of mankind recorded in Scripture and it led to Adam and Eve's fall from grace:

When the woman saw that the tree was good for food, and that it was a delight to the eyes, and that the tree was desirable to make one wise, she took from its fruit and ate; and she gave also to her husband with her, and he ate.

Genesis 3:6

The downward spiral into sin for Eve began when she started to observe the Tree of Knowledge of Good and Evil from her natural, or worldly, perspective. God had specifically commanded they could eat of any tree but the Tree of Knowledge of Good and Evil but Eve saw the tree was good for fruit, and pleasing to the eyes, and desirable for wisdom. Her focus left Jesus and His Words and centered on her own thoughts and the suggestions from Satan. Once that happened then her insights began to seem more wise than the clear instruction of God. It was only a matter of time as Eve contemplated the tree and relied on her own understanding that it led to her willful and deliberate disobedience. To this day mankind still struggles with the temptation to rely on our own understanding and worldly wisdom. This bent, or propensity to trust our own understanding must be constantly guarded against. We must also recognize it and combat it with the Word. Proverbs 3:5 instructs us to trust in the Lord and not lean, or rely on our own understanding:

> *It was only a matter of time as Eve contemplated the tree and relied on her own understanding that it led to her willful and deliberate disobedience.*

> *Trust in the LORD with all your heart And do not lean on your own understanding.*
> *Proverbs 3:5*

7 Ways to Increase the Wisdom of God in Your Life

Now let's look specifically at seven ways the Bible shows us how to increase in godly wisdom and instruction.

1. Asked for by Faith in God

The first step to receiving wisdom from God is to ask for it in faith. God does not want you to live in fear and worry because of lack of knowledge and according to James 1:5 has graciously invited you to ask Him in faith and has promised to give you all the wisdom you need:

But if any of you lacks wisdom, let him ask of God, who gives to all generously and without reproach, and it will be given to him.

James 1:5

Think about the different areas in your life that you desperately need God's wisdom in order to be successful and simply make right and good choices. Some examples are in areas of finances, career, marriage, parenting, and health. As you pray and think about these areas you need God's wisdom in write them down and be as specific as possible. For example, if you are experiencing conflict in parenting a child or teenager don't just ask God for wisdom in parenting, get specific. Ask God to give you patience when the child is uncooperative or to show you how to discipline in love and not anger or frustration. As you contemplate the specifics and nuances of your requests it will also allow the Holy Spirit to guide you in to knowing clearly what to ask for and how to focus your prayers. Focused and specific prayers become moments of rejoicing and faith building when God answers those prayers to the letter. Too often we generalize our prayers to the point that we fail to see the miracle of God's hand at work.

Focused and specific prayers become moments of rejoicing and faith building when God answers those prayers to the letter.

2.   *Led by the Holy Spirit*

"But when He, the Spirit of truth, comes, He will guide you into all the truth;

John 16:13

For the LORD gives wisdom; From His mouth come knowledge and understanding.

Proverbs 2:6

Once we have asked God in faith for wisdom then the key that unlocks the door to His revelation is knowing how to be led by the Holy Spirit. To be led by the Holy Spirit means to recognize when He is communicating with you, know what He is saying and to respond in faith and obedience. Refer to Chapter 4 for detailed instruction on how to hear and follow the Holy Spirit.

3. *Guided by the Word of God*

The Bible is a really big book with a lot of useful information. The Old Testament has thirty-nine books and the New Testament twenty-seven for a total of sixty-six books from Genesis to Revelation. Those sixty-six books are divided out into 1,189 chapters, and the chapters are comprised of 23,145 verses. If you read through the Bible out loud without stopping it would take you about 71 hours. At 15 minutes a day it can be read through in a year. All this being said, it can be an overwhelming task to find guidance and instruction from its pages if you are not familiar with its contents or do not have a plan and system for mining its gold.

But before we go further, never forget the Bible is much more than a well of useful information, or like the acronym B.I.B.L.E spells, Basic Instructions Before Leaving Earth. We cannot fall into the error of relegating the Bible to only a user's manual to be referred to when life has stumped us. Even the sinner does as such and receives the reward of wisdom. It is much more than a quality of life enhancer. When we probe its pages we should not be searching for a solution but for a Savior. The Scripture declares they are *"inspired by God"* literally, God-breathed. They were words on the lips of God before they were penned by the hand of man. We would do well to stop reading the Bible

We cannot fall into the error of relegating the Bible to only a user's manual to be referred to when life has stumped us. Even the sinner does as such and receives the reward of wisdom.

all together, *"for the letter kills"*. *(2 Cor. 3:6)* I stopped reading the Bible years ago when I heard a Catholic priest say he stopped reading the Bible. He had my attention since I was listening to his series on how to study the Bible. He went on to say the Bible is God's words and when he stopped "reading" words and started "listening" for His voice it revolutionized his relationship with God and His Word. When reading for content or answers becomes our first priority we miss out on the primary purpose of the Bible, to reveal Jesus and build a relationship to Him and with Him.

When we turn to the Scriptures for guidance we should first focus our attention on the Speaker of the Bible. Ask the Holy Spirit to speak to you as you search the Scriptures. The Holy Spirit is your personal Counselor and Guide to all Truth. (John 16:13) When you approach the Scriptures with your ears before your eyes then you are well on your way to finding what you are searching for.

When you approach the Scriptures with your ears before your eyes then you are well on your way to finding what you are searching for.

Most of the answers and wisdom the Bible offers is based on general principles of godly living. For example, you're not going to find the direct answer to who you should marry in the Bible, but you will find what kind of spouse a person should be looking for or be. The Bible can't tell you whether to invest your money in stocks or start a business but it does have much to say on wise financial decisions and practices.

The person who has a clear word from the Lord is confident that what God has revealed to them by His Spirit will manifest in the natural, so they act by faith accordingly.

I suggest you invest in a good topical Bible to help you search the Scriptures for subjects related to your need. Some study Bibles also have good subject indexes to assist you in your search.

But a good subject index in the back of your Bible is not the entire solution for direction and decision making. As I said before, there are many important questions we have that aren't specifically addressed in Scripture. Questions such as, Where should I go to school? What city should I live in? What kind of car should I buy? Who should I vote for in the next presidential primary? Can I trust my child with a new babysitter? Is my teenager telling me the truth? These questions and many more like them are often the kind that we wrestle with. Often the general principles the Bible gives can go very far in narrowing down our choices and eliminating poor choices. But still, even then, sometimes we are left with an either/or decision. Can we search the Bible for answers to these questions? If so, how do we search the Scriptures for answers that aren't explicitly there?

The more assured we are we have clearly heard from God the less opportunity Satan has to sow doubt and cause us to be hesitant and uncertain, or double-minded, in our obedience.

These types of questions are revealed by the Spirit in the presence of Jesus as the next step explains.

4.   *Revealed in the Presence of Jesus*

Just as Moses received instruction while in the presence of God it is a pattern and example for us to follow as well. No wisdom this world has to offer compares to the heavenly wisdom and knowledge in Christ. Paul taught this reality in his letter to Colossia:

> *that is, Christ Himself, in whom are hidden all the treasures of wisdom and knowledge.*
>
> *Colossians 2:2,3*

Truth is in Jesus and no other. Paul goes onto tell the church in Ephesus:

> *if indeed you have heard Him and have been taught in Him, just as truth is in Jesus,*
>
> *Ephesians 4:21*

When you bask in the presence of Jesus and set as his feet He will impart and release wisdom and understanding into your heart. He desires to give you all the wisdom and instruction you need to make the right choices in order to live an abundant and victorious life. As you practice the presence of God and spend time consistently and continually in the Spirit you will develop an assurance in hearing from Him and that will increase your confidence and authority as you walk it out in obedience. The more assured we are we have clearly heard from God the less opportunity Satan has to sow doubt and cause us to be hesitant and uncertain, or double-minded, in our obedience. Satan has been shooting his fiery darts of doubt beginning in the Garden of Eden in Genesis 2 when he used it to question God's command to Eve, *"Has God said?..."*

It is so important that you get a clear word from the Lord before making major decisions. Wait on the Lord and be patient. Don't rush it and don't step out in blind faith either. The faith that is pleasing to God is not blind. According to

Sadly many Christians have stepped out in blind faith hoping to do great things for God and failed miserably because God never told them to do it!

Hebrews: *"faith is the assurance of things hoped for, the conviction of things not seen." (Heb. 11:1)* Stepping out in faith is acting upon the conviction and truth that you have heard from the Lord. The King James Version translates conviction as "evidence". In the natural you may not see the answer or solution but that's not your evidence or proof to step out in faith. Your conviction to act by faith comes from the fact you have heard from God on the matter! There is nothing blind in it! It is that kind of faith that builds a sturdy shield to deflect all the fiery doubt darts from the enemy. The person who has a clear word from the Lord is confident that what God has revealed to them by His Spirit will manifest in the natural, so they act by faith accordingly.

Let me illustrate by giving two different real life examples that contrast the difference between blind faith and faith based on hearing the voice of God. Recently a young man called me to discuss some choices he needed to make concerning following God into ministry. He was at a place where he felt he might need to move to another town which would mean quitting a good job he currently had and moving to a part of the state that would be much more difficult to find similar employment opportunities. But he wanted to be in ministry so bad! And wasn't quitting his job and moving to pursue ministry a just cause and admirable act of faith? He was at an impasse and didn't have any clear direction. He expressed that to step out and do it was by itself an act of faith and maybe the course to take, he just wasn't sure. I listened to him and I knew he genuinely wanted to make the right choice and please God. Now before I tell you what I said to him understand that following the will of God is not solely based on employment opportunities or quitting a good job. That was not the major issue in his predicament. He was precariously close to stepping out in blind faith with the assumption that isn't that what God would probably want? He had not heard from God one way or the other. He had no conviction or proof from God to step out in faith because God had not revealed to him what to do. Sadly many Christians have stepped out in blind faith hoping to do great things for God and failed miserably because God never told them to do it! In Matthew 4 Jesus did not jump off the cliff because the Scripture said God gives His angels charge over us, He didn't jump off the cliff because it came as a temptation from Satan and not a clear command from His Father! Thank the Lord the young man continued to be patient and press in for direction from the Holy Spirit.

In contrast to blind faith is faith based on a clear conviction from God. I have a good friend who was recently a pastor at a local church. God began to stir in his heart a desire to leave and pursue full-time missionary work in a country on another continent. He had a good position at a church where the people loved him and provided for him and his wife. The country where he was feeling the call to offered very little concrete answers or direction—there were a lot of unknowns. But he did not rush the process but regularly poured out his heart to God and laid his petitions before the Throne. Over the course of months God began to give him Scriptures that confirmed what he was feeling in his heart was truly from God. When he did call me for prayer he shared those Scriptures with me and the conversations he had had with His Heavenly Father. As he spoke to me I could sense the faith that God had been building within him. The time finally did arrive where he had to step out in faith. He had to quit his pastorate and launch out into the next phase of ministry God had for him and although there were times his flesh wanted to respond in worry or fear his decision was based upon the clear conviction and evidences God had already deposited in his heart through His word. He is currently two months serving as a missionary in a foreign country and God is miraculously using him to advance the Kingdom!

It is in the presence of Jesus that He brings confirmation through His Word concerning decisions in our life. Seek to hear clear instruction from God and that will become your confidence and light to carry you through the deep waters and dark valleys to your promised land.

5. Received From the Prayers of Others

The first four ways we receive instruction and wisdom from God is of a personal nature between you and God. But the next three ways, the fifth, sixth and seventh, are fundamentally different and require us to depend upon our fellow brothers and sisters in Christ. Even though, we must still take their influences before Christ that He may confirm the truth.

The fifth way to grow in wisdom is through the prayers of others. Notice in the following two Scriptures how the Apostle Paul prayed for the church at Ephesus and also at Colossia:

> that the God of our Lord Jesus Christ, the Father of glory, may give to you a spirit of wisdom and of revelation in the knowledge of Him.
>
> Ephesians 1:17

For this reason also, since the day we heard of it, we have not ceased to pray for you and to ask that you may be filled with the knowledge of His will in all spiritual wisdom and understanding,

Colossians 1:9-10

The Apostle Paul continuously prayed that God would give them supernatural wisdom, revelation, knowledge and understanding to know Christ more fully and His will for their lives. Not only can we and should we make those prayers for ourselves and loved ones but we should recruit and encourage others to pray for us as well!

Daniel asked for time to reveal the dream and immediately went to his intercessory group, Shadrach, Meshach and Abed-nego and asked them to pray for him that God would reveal to him the king's dream. Who do you have praying for you?

The prophet Daniel in the Old Testament understood and applied the power of mutual intercession for wisdom. In Daniel 2, King Nebuchadnezzar ordered all the wise men to be executed because they were unable to tell him his dream. Daniel asked for time to reveal the dream and immediately went to his intercessory group, Shadrach, Meshach and Abed-nego and asked them to pray for him that God would reveal to him the king's dream. Who do you have praying for you?

6. Conferred Through Spiritual Leaders

An often overlooked and underutilized avenue to increased heavenly wisdom that God has ordained is through the laying on of hands by godly ministers who flow in the gifts of the Spirit. There are Old and New Testament Biblical examples of this to consider. Let's start in the Old Testament with Moses and Joshua:

Now Joshua the son of Nun was filled with the spirit of wisdom, for Moses had laid his hands on him; and the sons of Israel listened to him and did as the LORD had commanded Moses.

Deuteronomy 34:9

Moses was Joshua's commander and leader but he was also a type of pastor to Joshua and the Israelites. In this example God had Moses lay hands and anoint Joshua with the spirit of wisdom. This wasn't the first time Moses had done something like this. In Numbers chapter 11 Moses was overwhelmed with the task and responsibilities of leading the people and cried out to the Lord in desperation. The Lord heard Moses' cries and directed him to select and bring seventy men to gather around the Tabernacle. It was there that the Scripture says:

"Then the LORD came down in the cloud and spoke to him; and He took of the Spirit who was upon him and placed Him upon the seventy elders. And when the Spirit rested upon them, they prophesied. But they did not do it again.

Numbers 11:25

Rather than anointing the seventy separately God specifically *"took of the Spirit who was upon [Moses] and placed Him [the Spirit] upon the seventy elders."* This anointing was an anointing of wisdom and leadership for the task of judging and leading the people.

In the New Testament the Apostle Paul greatly desired to see the church at Rome so he could impart to them spiritual gifts. According to 1 Corinthians 12 there are at least nine spiritual gifts listed and two of them are the word of wisdom and the word of knowledge. How acutely do we need godly and anointed ministers; apostles, prophets, evangelists, pastor and teachers, who are full of wisdom and the Spirit to lay hands on the body and impart supernatural gifts of wisdom and knowledge! Who do you know that could lay hands on you?

7. *Collected Through Godly Counsel*

Another and often used method of attaining instruction is to proactively glean it from those more experienced and wise than yourself. There are many Biblical references to seeking wise counsel here are just a couple to consider:

> *The way of a fool is right in his own eyes, But a wise man is he who listens to counsel.*
>
> *Proverbs 12:15*

> *Listen to counsel and accept discipline, That you may be wise the rest of your days. Many plans are in a man's heart, But the counsel of the LORD will stand.*
>
> *Proverbs 19:20-21*

Be diligent in seeking out wisdom from others, whether that be people, books or conferences. Don't let pride keep you from asking the questions you have. Speak up and ask that question because it's better to ask and be considered a fool for a moment than to keep silent and remain a fool forever.

Once you have adequately searched and collected counsel then you must take everything before God and ask Him to confirm your findings and give you His stamp of approval. Too often many go on a fact finding mission and collect a lot of good advice but fail to lay their findings at the feet of Jesus so He can show them the best way to proceed.

Speak up and ask that question because it's better to ask and be considered a fool for a moment than to keep silent and remain a fool forever.

On the mountain in the Presence of God Moses received supernatural revelation and instruction on how to lead the people. That is the place where you too can expect God to give you instruction and wisdom for living life to the fullest. It is in His presence you are able to clearly and confidently hear His voice. God has given you at least seven ways to receive heavenly instruction. May you be diligent to pursue all that God has for you.

7 Ways to Increase the Wisdom of God in Your Life

1. Asked for by Faith in God
2. Led by the Holy Spirit
3. Guided by the Word of God
4. Revealed in the Presence of Jesus
5. Received From the Prayers of Others
6. Conferred Through Spiritual Leaders
7. Collected Through Godly Counsel

Come Rest!

Then Moses went up to the mountain, and the cloud covered the mountain. The glory of the LORD rested on Mount Sinai, and the cloud covered it for six days;

Exodus 24:15,16a

Come to Me, all who are weary and heavy-laden, and I will give you rest. Take My yoke upon you and learn from Me, for I am gentle and humble in heart, and YOU WILL FIND REST FOR YOUR SOULS.

Matthew 11:28-29

And He said, "My presence shall go with you, and I will give you rest."

Exodus 33:14

He makes me lie down in green pastures; He leads me beside quiet waters. He restores my soul; He guides me in the paths of righteousness For His name's sake.

Psalms 23:2-3

10

Regeneration

The time had finally arrived for Moses to meet God! Moses left the elders behind and taking only Joshua, his personal assistant, with him trekked further up the mountain. But instead of a much anticipated, eagerly expecting God encounter, he waits six whole days enveloped in the Glory cloud before God calls to Him to come up one more time . Why did God make Moses wait six days? It is likely Moses needed to decompress, to rest and recover from all that had just transpired. Moses needed to still and rest his mind, spirit and body to prepare for the presence of God. It's not an accident Joshua was still with him. This was a much needed time for Moses to relax and reflect on the amazing miracles, experiences and difficulties he had just endured.

Moses Had Come a Long Way

A Hebrew slave gave birth to Moses during a time when Pharaoh feared the Hebrew slaves were going to outnumber their Egyptian taskmasters so to control their numbers he issued a decree that all male babies born by Hebrew women be executed. Moses' mother nursed him until he was too big to hide and then fashioned a basket from the reeds along the bank of the Nile, placed the baby inside and floated him down the river, instructing his older sister to follow. By divine intervention, the basket was discovered by one of Pharaoh's daughters who drew him from the water and raised him as her own. For the first forty years of Moses' life he was raised in the Egyptian royal court and afforded all the education and luxuries of one related to Pharaoh.

Around the age of forty he killed an Egyptian slave master who was beating a Hebrew slave and then fled for his life into the desert. For the next forty years Moses tended sheep on the back side of the desert and it was there where God appeared to him in the burning bush and called him to return to Egypt and demand the release of the Hebrews. During this time he had settled down, married, was raising a family and working the family business to which he had married into: herding sheep. Relatively speaking, this was a calm and restful season in the life of Moses. That all changed upon accepting his call from God and returning to Egypt to confront the Pharaoh with the command from God, "Let my people go!"

To facilitate the presence of God in our lives it is important to make opportunities to rest our mind, body and spirit. It took Moses six days of rest before his God encounter.

It is estimated there were from 500,000 to over 1 million men, women and children that followed Moses out of Egypt. Think about it for a moment, for forty years prior Moses had been a shepherd of sheep spending a solitary existence responsible only for protecting and leading a herd of sheep to the next grassy knoll or spring of water. Now he was responsible for a nation of people with all their men, women and children depending on him. He definitely needed some alone time to gather himself and rest before God called him up into His presence.

There is a powerful principle here for us to consider. To facilitate the presence of God in our lives it is important to make opportunities to rest our mind, body and spirit. It took Moses six days of rest before his God encounter.

God Commands Us to Rest

The commandment to rest is so important that it comes in at number four on the top 10 list of commandments that God gave Moses on the mountain top, or most familiarly known as the Ten Commandments:

> *"Remember the sabbath day, to keep it holy.*
>
> *Exodus 20:8*

God modeled the importance of rest, even though He is all powerful and does not slumber or sleep (Ps. 1221:4), after the six days of creation:

> *By the seventh day God completed His work which He had done, and He rested on the seventh day from all His work which He had done. Then God blessed the seventh day and sanctified it, because in it He rested from all His work which God had created and made.*
>
> *Genesis 2:2-3*

On the seventh day God stepped back from the works of His hands, the universe He had birthed from His infinite mind, and took the time to admire and reflect on the beauty of His creation. He recognized the majesty, immenseness, order, variety and complexity of the universe reflected those very qualities of Himself and the work of His hands,

To rest is more than refraining from work or pausing activities but the commandment to rest is a command to rest in God, to be in His presence, to be at peace in God as well as with God.

all created things seen and unseen would declare His glory for all eternity. In His unlimited wisdom He commanded that man should also rest, take a break from his work, and reflect on the goodness and power of God in his own life. That man should recognize his complete dependence on God and without Him he is nothing. That man's greatest purpose is to rest in God and enjoy Him forever. To rest is more than refraining from work or pausing activities but the commandment to rest is a command to rest in God, to be in His presence, to be at peace in God as well as with God.

There is a rest that can only come from the Throne Room, it is a supernatural rest that the world cannot provide-for the world has no answer, nor any desire to take your burdens. No amount of sleep or vacation can restore a soul laden down with cares and worries and the burdens of life. Only in the presence of God is there fullness of joy and the joy of the Lord is your strength. *"And He said, "My presence shall go with you, and I will give you rest." (Ex. 33:14)*

And so God calls to you give Him your burdens, to find rest for your soul. *"Cast all your anxiety on Him, because He cares for you" (1 Pet. 5:7)* Stop seeking the temporary comforts and empty promises the world offers and come rest in Jesus:

> *Stop seeking the temporary comforts and empty promises the world offers and come rest in Jesus.*

> *Come to Me, all who are weary and heavy-laden, and I will give you rest. Take My yoke upon you and learn from Me, for I am gentle and humble in heart, and YOU WILL FIND REST FOR YOUR SOULS.*
>
> *Matthew 11:28-29*

Living Above the Mosquito Line

There are certain villages and cities in Africa that have far fewer malaria outbreaks in comparison to population centers in close proximity simply because they are at a higher elevation. At a certain height in elevation the climate, temperature and seasonal weather restrict the activity and proliferation of the mosquito therefore reducing the chances of a person contracting the deadly malaria disease from an infected mosquito bite. The same can be said for poisonous snakes and tics. When you're hiking up a mountain at eight or ten thousand feet above sea level you have far fewer chances at getting struck by a rattle snake or picking up a tic than if you are at the base of the mountain hiking through the valley. When we pursue the presence of God and strike up the spiritual mountain it adds another level of protection from temptations, spiritual attacks and the pressures of the daily grind that try to poison us like a rattler, pester us like a determined mosquito, or latch on like a tic and suck the life blood out of us.

Rest Builds Muscle

For body builders rest is as important as lifting weights to build muscle mass. Actually, muscles don't grow in the gym they grow in recovery after the workouts. Weight lifting breaks down the muscle fibers and it is during the recovery or rest cycle that the body repairs and builds up the muscle fibers which increases the mass and size of the muscle. If a weight lifter works out the same muscles every day and takes no days off to rest eventually they will reach a plateau and stop seeing results for all their effort and time.

The spiritual parallels are exactly the same. Growth for the believer takes place in the presence of Jesus. Spiritual growth, or maturity, is not measured by your birth date—the year you got saved, but rather by the time you have spent on the mountain soaking in Jesus. That is why a person can have been saved for thirty years and still be an infant in Christ but a person only one or two years in the faith can be well on their way to a strong mature walk with God. The former has just been circling the mountain their whole life and the latter has been hiking to the top. One is a valley dweller and the other a mountain climber.

Spiritual growth, or maturity, is not measured by your birth date—the year you got saved, but rather by the time you have spent on the mountain soaking in Jesus.

Jesus Took Time to Rest

Jesus modeled to us the extreme importance of spiritual retreats during his ministry on earth. Luke records he *"would often slip away to the wilderness and pray." (Luke 5:16)* This was not a once in a while or in time of great need activity but a habit *"he would often"* Jesus practiced and the disciples took notice.

Mark noticed this habit of Jesus too and mentions:

> *In the early morning, while it was still dark, Jesus got up, left the house, and went away to a secluded place, and was praying there.*
>
> *Mark 1:35*

Resting in the Lord is something that we must fight for and make happen in our jam packed lives. It means pressing in to the presence of God and once there not leaving until we have received a fresh infilling of His presence into our life that rejuvenates, renews and empowers our spirit within us. The benefit we receive from resting is God is similar to plugging a cell phone into a charger. In His presence we are energized and strengthened. Just as we daily charge our phone so should we daily plug in to Jesus. The Bible declares the joy of the Lord is our strength. (Neh. 8:10) In His presence our joy is renewed in Him and from that comes supernatural energy to sustain us.

The Prophet Habakkuk knew the power of waiting and watching:

> *I will stand on my guard post And station myself on the rampart; And I will keep watch to see what He will speak to me, And how I may reply when I am reproved.*
>
> *Habakkuk 2:1*

The Prophet Habakkuk climbed a rampart or guard tower to get alone with God in order to hear from Him. That was his way of escaping the hustle and bustle of every day life and retreating to a place of solitude and silence in order to press in to the presence of God.

Take Spiritual Retreats

Planning and participating in your own personal spiritual retreat is a very empowering activity. By necessity, sometimes those retreats are limited to early mornings and stealing away an hour here or there and getting no further away than a park bench or car seat but don't undervalue those moments. With practice and consistency you will begin to depend and eagerly anticipate those precious moments with your Lord. But there also should be times when you carve out an overnight or weekend and plan a spiritual retreat away from your common surroundings. It doesn't have to be expensive either. Just last month I spent a couple nights in the spare bedroom of a good friend of mine who lives in a small rural town. I told him my purpose and he and his wife were overjoyed to be able to open their home to me for my spiritual retreat. In the mornings I took long walks by an old cemetery and reflected on the goodness of God and in the evenings sat on the back porch amazed by the glory of the stars that shone so brightly in the absence of city lights.

There have been other times I planned a trip to the coast for the one purpose of seeking God and resting in His presence. There is something about walking the beach in the morning before sunrise, hearing the waves crash, smelling and feeling the salty breeze on your face and the cool wet sand between your toes that can rapture a person right into the holy of holies, right to the top of the mountain and into the presence of God. Be sure to take a journal and record all your thoughts, feelings and impressions you will receive during these intimate moments. Those journal entries will be food for your soul long after the retreat is over. Weeks, months, even years later when you go back and read those journal entries you will be taken back to that moment and God will rekindle that revelation He gave to you and you will be encouraged and renewed by it all over again.

Ascending the Mountain of God

Moses rested and waited six days before God called to him from the cloud. The mountain was a place of refuge and rest. God has modeled and commanded we rest in Him. As our Good Shepherd He leads us to opportunities to rest our weary souls:

> *He makes me lie down in green pastures; He leads me beside quiet waters. He restores my soul; He guides me in the paths of righteousness For His name's sake.*
>
> *Psalms 23:2-3*

It is when we have rested and been restored in the Presence of God that we can be set aflame as now He calls us to Come Burn!

Come Burn!

And to the eyes of the sons of Israel the appearance of the glory of the LORD was like a consuming fire on the mountain top.

Exodus 24:17

It came about when Moses was coming down from Mount Sinai (and the two tablets of the testimony were in Moses' hand as he was coming down from the mountain), that Moses did not know that the skin of his face shone because of his speaking with Him.

Exodus 34:29

Therefore, since we receive a kingdom which cannot be shaken, let us show gratitude, by which we may offer to God an acceptable service with reverence and awe; for our God is a consuming fire.

Hebrews 12:28-29

and [Jesus] *led them up on a high mountain by themselves. And He was transfigured before them; and His face shone like the sun, and His garments became as white as light.

Matthew 17:1-2

And there appeared to them tongues as of fire distributing themselves, and they rested on each one of them. And they were all filled with the Holy Spirit...

Acts 2:3-4

11

Consummation

Glow sticks are fun and entertaining for kids and adults alike. They work on a very simple process. Essentially they are a small portable chemistry experiment. When you bend the glow stick until you hear the cracking on the inside you have broken a small fragile glass vial. That inner vial releases hydrogen peroxide that activates the surrounding solution through a chemical reaction which causes the stick to glow.

A glow stick won't glow until the inner chamber is broken and the hydrogen peroxide released. There is a spiritual parallel and principle to be learned here, before God can use you, before you can burn and glow for Christ, you must be broken. Humility breaks the pride in our hearts that releases the Spirit of God to interact with our spirit and sparks the glow for Christ. In other words, when you humble and submit your will and desires to His will, and in humility walk in obedience to His word, it breaks pride and selfish ambition

A glow stick won't glow until the inner chamber is broken and the hydrogen peroxide released. There is a spiritual parallel and principle to be learned here, before God can use us, before we can burn and glow for Christ, we must be broken.

that keeps you from connecting and releasing the presence of God in your life.

At the moment of salvation, God comes into your life to live, but you still have your will and pride that must be continually submitted to the will of God. God will allow struggles and challenges that bend you, and as long as you resist and try to do things your way, your pride and selfishness stay intact. And like that glass vial that holds the hydrogen peroxide and separates it from the solution, so our pride and self-will separates our spirit from fully interacting and releasing the light and pervading presence of God into the world around us.

God is a Consuming Fire

> And to the eyes of the sons of Israel the appearance of the glory of the LORD was like a consuming fire on the mountain top.
>
> Exodus 24:17

It was not the first time, nor by coincidence, that God chose to manifest Himself as fire to the sons of Israel. His first appearance as a fire was to the Patriarch Abraham when He passed between the animal sacrifices as a smoking oven and flaming torch. (Gen. 15:17) He appeared to Moses as fire that did not consume the bush. (Ex. 3:2) He led them up out of Egypt as a pillar of fire by night. (Ex. 13:21) And now as Moses entered the Cloud to the Hebrews at the foot of Mt. Sinai it looked as if the mountain had exploded into a blazing torch.

Moses Had a Sonburn

One of the physical manifestations of Moses' time in the presence of God was it caused his face to literally glow. Back in chapter six we discussed that these visitations of God had to be pre-incarnate manifestations of Jesus. Moses was talking with the Son of God and the result was he got a sonburn!

Ascending the Mountain of God

It came about when Moses was coming down from Mount Sinai (and the two tablets of the testimony were in Moses' hand as he was coming down from the mountain), that Moses did not know that the skin of his face shone because of his speaking with Him.

Exodus 34:29

The Old Testament often uses physical, or natural, experiences to point us to spiritual, or supernatural realities. What could it mean to us as New Testament believers to know that Moses' face glowed as a direct result of being in the presence of God? It's not an accident or coincidence that just his faced glowed and not his entire body or any other part of him. Moses' face glowed, a physical manifestation of God's glory, to show us that when we are in His presence we too supernaturally become more and more like Him. And our glow, the effect of us in His presence, should cause others to take notice we have just come down from the mountain top.

> *Moses' face glowed, a physical manifestation of God's glory, to show us that when we are in His presence we too supernaturally become more and more like Him.*

Later Moses had to place a veil over his face because his glow disturbed the people:

So when Aaron and all the sons of Israel saw Moses, behold, the skin of his face shone, and they were afraid to come near him.

But whenever Moses went in before the LORD to speak with Him, he would take off the veil until he came out; and whenever he came out and spoke to the sons of Israel what he had been commanded, the sons of Israel would see the face of Moses, that the skin of Moses' face shone. So Moses would replace the veil over his face until he went in to speak with Him.

Exodus 34:30, 34-35

Don't be surprised when you come down off the mountain top burning brightly with passion and zeal for God that it has the same consequences it did for Moses. Your love and enthusiasm for the things of God will seldom be met with equal fervor. Not everyone wants or understands the life of one committed to Christ and continually basking in His presence. It is a disturbing reminder to them of their compromise and neglect of Jesus in their own life. If they are not convicted and inspired by you to pursue Jesus for themselves then they have resisted the calling of the Holy Spirit and out of their flesh they will respond in agitation and anger. They will accuse you of being holier than thou, or call you a fanatic, or patronize you with false enthusiasm. They will outwardly smile and nod as you radiate the love of God and express your devotion to Him and secretly they will yearn for the moment you leave to spew venom and gossip about you in your absence. When this happens, don't be alarmed, it happened to Jesus:

> *For to you it has been granted for Christ's sake, not only to believe in Him, but also to suffer for His sake,*
>
> *Philippians 1:29*

When Jesus became human He was the perfect representation of God. He loved perfectly and completely. If Jesus loved everyone with a perfect love and made enemies that eventually had Him executed don't be surprised when your expression of love for God, expressed through an imperfect, error prone nature, brings upon you persecution from brothers and sisters in the Lord. Be encouraged, those persecutions are building up for you eternal rewards in Heaven. When you walk the path Christ walked, and suffer for His Name, you will be rewarded if you just don't give up.

Jesus Radiated Light

The Bible says, *"God is light and in him there is no darkness." (1 Jn. 1:5)* The glory of Jesus emanated from Him as bright as sun light when He revealed His true glory and was transformed before Peter, James and John on the mountain top:

> *Six days later Jesus *took with Him Peter and James and John his brother, and *led them up on a high mountain by themselves. And He was transfigured before them; and His face shone like the sun, and His garments became as white as light. And behold, Moses and Elijah appeared to them, talking with Him.*
>
> Matthew 17:1-3

Now you can have a better understanding of why Moses' face glowed when he came out of the tent of meeting. He was talking with Jesus before He came to earth as a man. As a man, the glory of Jesus was covered in skin. On top of the mountain when he was transfigured before them, He released His glory to a measure the men could behold and not be struck dead. When Jesus was in the tent with Moses He did not have flesh and blood to cover Him so His glory covered Him and the light that animated from His Being caused Moses' face to glow from His glory. When you spend time in the presence of Jesus and saturate yourself in His glory, the glory of God will permeate your personality and people will see the glory of God upon you. It may not be a literal glow but your countenance and face will be glowing nonetheless.

Satan's greatest fear, his phobia, is a person on fire for God for they operate in power and authority and do not tolerate his lies and activity.

Holy Spirit and Fire

Up to now we have mostly equated fire with passion but to be consumed by God is more than to be flowing in passion. What is the fire that the church so desperately needs in this generation? It is a fire that consumes the believer with passion, boldness, intensity, motivation and energy for God to live in Him and for Him. It fuels a boldness to live unashamedly for Christ and to declare the Gospel in power. It is a fire that intensifies and clarifies with laser focus godly focus. It is a fire that motivates and energizes the believer to press in and through adversities. It is a fire that consumes dead works and selfish ambitions. It is a fire that is contagious and spreads revival to a dry and barren world. Satan's greatest fear, his phobia, is a person on fire for God, for they operate in power and authority and do not tolerate his lies and activity. Satan acts like a forest ranger, scanning the terrain looking for the smallest spark and passion for God to snuff out. He wants to smother passion before it rages into an inferno and engulfs others into the Kingdom of God, spreading revival throughout the land and destroying the works of the devil.

What Can We Do if the Ember has Grown Cold?

Let's be clear, the fire can not be fabricated or drummed up through a special formula or through natural means. Where does this fire come from? How can we burn with passion and zeal for the things of God? What can we do if the ember has grown cold? Of course, the fire is fanned on the mountain top in His presence, but let's be even more specific. The fire we speak of is supernatural and must come from Heaven. The fire comes when one is Spirit-baptized—completely immersed, and in the context of fire, engulfed and filled with the Holy Spirit. Notice what John the Baptist said about fire baptism:

> "As for me, I baptize you with water for repentance, but He who is coming after me is mightier than I, and I am not fit to remove His sandals; He will baptize you with the Holy Spirit and fire.
>
> Matthew 3:11

The baptism of John was one of water that pointed to the cleansing of the heart through repentance leading to salvation. But the baptism of Jesus by the Holy Spirit in fire also speaks of a cleansing, but not unto salvation, but one of purification and a burning away of all that is natural, worldly and temporary, so that all that is supernatural and eternal may

In the furnace of the Holy Spirit He burns away fear, insecurities, false identities, failures, mistakes and strongholds so that we may run with confidence the race set before us.

remain. In the furnace of the Holy Spirit He burns away fear, insecurities, false identities, failures, mistakes and strongholds so that you may run with confidence the race set before you. Believers know of John's baptism of water and its symbolizing repentance unto salvation but few grasp the necessity of fire baptism: a baptism not for salvation but one for the manifested supernatural power from the Holy Spirit. In water baptism, we are buried with Christ and come up a brand new creation, a vessel and temple prepared to carry the anointing of God. In Spirit baptism, we are engulfed in the fire of the Holy Spirit and come up energized or endowed with God-infused power to be a living testimony and expression of the will and heart of the Baptizer.

Be Filled With the Spirit!

Jesus repeatedly taught the disciples that He would leave and send to them the Helper, the Holy Spirit:

> "But I tell you the truth, it is to your advantage that I go away; for if I do not go away, the Helper will not come to you; but if I go, I will send Him to you.
> John 16:7

He taught them that the Holy Spirit was a gift from the Father and theirs for the asking:

"If you then, being evil, know how to give good gifts to your children, how much more will your heavenly Father give the Holy Spirit to those who ask Him?"

Luke 11:13

He also taught them what to expect when the Holy Spirit came upon them:

"But when He, the Spirit of truth, comes, He will guide you into all the truth; for He will not speak on His own initiative, but whatever He hears, He will speak; and He will disclose to you what is to come.

John 16:13

Before He ascended into the clouds He told them they were going to be filled with the promise of the Father, the gift of the Holy Spirit:

for John baptized with water, but you will be baptized with the Holy Spirit not many days from now."

Acts 1:5

And just a few verses later, He explained that the Holy Spirit would give them power to be witnesses:

but you will receive power when the Holy Spirit has come upon you; and you shall be My witnesses both in Jerusalem, and in all Judea and Samaria, and even to the remotest part of the earth."

Acts 1:8

And as promised, Jesus did send the Holy Spirit, as recorded in Acts 2. And it is no surprise the Holy Spirit manifested Himself as a flame that rested, or engulfed, each one of them:

When the day of Pentecost had come, they were all together in one place. And suddenly there came from heaven a noise like a violent rushing wind, and it filled the whole house where they were sitting. And there appeared to them tongues as of fire distributing themselves, and they rested on each one of them. And they were all filled with the Holy Spirit and began to speak with other tongues, as the Spirit was giving them utterance.

Acts 2:1-4

> The gift of the Holy Spirit is a special supernatural infusion that sets our passions on fire and empowers us with a fresh infilling of His Presence.

If you desire to be consumed by God then you must first be filled with the Holy Spirit. The infilling of the Holy Spirit is promised to all who believe and ask the Father. The Father is the gift-giver, the Son is the Baptizer and the Holy Spirit is the gift. Being filled with the Holy Spirit is not just a one time event. He comes to dwell within us at salvation and promises to never leave us but we are commanded to ask for the gift of the Holy Spirit, a special supernatural infusion, that sets our passions on fire and empowers us with a fresh infilling of His Presence.

Do you want to be consumed in God? Then be filled with His Holy Spirit! Do you want the supernatural reality of the presence of God upon your life empowering, energizing, leading, revealing, purifying and helping you? Then be filled with the Holy Spirit! If your heart is quickened within you and you desire to be fire baptized in the Holy Spirit then pray with me now.

Lord,

I need you and your dwelling presence in my life. I want all that you have promised for me in your Word. Thank you for giving your Holy Spirit to those who ask. I ask for your Holy

*Spirit to fill me. Fill me with your presence and power to
live the supernatural and abundant life you have called me
to live. Lord, send the fire! Fall afresh on me. Consume all
that is not of you and release your power and passion upon
me today. I believe your Word. I receive the gift of the Holy
Spirit into my life today. Thank you for filling me with your
Holy Spirit and fire.*

In Jesus Name,

Amen.

This is not a one time prayer because being filled with the Holy
Spirit is not a one time event. Ephesians commands we are to *"...be
filled with the Spirit,"*. *(Eph. 5:18)* The verb "filled" in Greek means a
continual ever present and ongoing filling. Continue to meditate on
the Scriptures in this chapter that teach you about the reality and
necessity of the Holy Spirit. Make them your prayer, believe them,
ask the Holy Spirit to daily fill you and by faith believe you have
received Him!

Moses was baptized in fire while he communed with God on
the mountain top. When he came down off the mountain his face
glowed. You can not be in the Presence of God and not be changed and
conformed into His likeness. We have journeyed all the way to the top
of the mountain and only one more step remains. Let us boldly accept
the final call of God to Come Dwell!

*Therefore, since we receive a kingdom which cannot be
shaken, let us show gratitude, by which we may offer to
God an acceptable service with reverence and awe; for our
God is a consuming fire.*

Hebrews 12:28-29

Come Dwell!

and on the seventh day He called to Moses from the midst of the cloud... Moses entered the midst of the cloud as he went up to the mountain; and Moses was on the mountain forty days and forty nights

Exodus 24:16,18

For you have made the LORD, my refuge, Even the Most High, your dwelling place.

Psalm 91:9

God is known in Judah; His name is great in Israel. His tabernacle is in Salem; His dwelling place also is in Zion.

Psalm 76:1-2

The LORD roars from Zion And utters His voice from Jerusalem, And the heavens and the earth tremble. But the LORD is a refuge for His people And a stronghold to the sons of Israel. Then you will know that I am the LORD your God, Dwelling in Zion, My holy mountain.

Joel 3:16-17

12

Habitation

*and on the seventh day He called to Moses from the midst
of the cloud... Moses entered the midst of the cloud as he
went up to the mountain; and Moses was on the mountain
forty days and forty nights*

Exodus 24:16,18

Moses finally answered the call of God to come up and leaving
Joshua behind he ascended alone into the Glory Cloud. That
same call and invitation is for you too. God is calling you to come up
and dwell in His presence. To answer that call will require you to make
some serious adjustments in your life. You may have to rearrange your
calendar, cancel an appointment, delegate a responsibility so you can
get alone with God...a few hours, a few days, whatever it takes. There
are times for spiritual retreats with the masses; a Women's Retreat, a
Promise Keepers Convention. Then there are times you go with a select
few; your inner circle, your best friend, your spouse. And then there are
times where you leave everyone and everything behind and go it alone.

There is a Cost to Count

I participated in an ordination service at my church where we had
the honor of ordaining nine ministerial candidates. There was much

pomp and circumstance and I was asked to wear a yoke, or collar, for the occasion. I had never worn a yoke before, and to make matters worse, it was hot and the shirt collar was too tight around my neck. I got the bright idea to unbutton the button behind the yoke to give me a little relief. Ten minutes later I stood behind the pulpit to welcome the large crowd of people for the occasion. As I was speaking one of the ministerial candidates caught my eye and pointed at his neck. For a moment it didn't register. A minute later another person did the same. Then it clicked. I put my hand to my neck and my white yoke on my all black shirt was sticking half out waiting for the slightest tug to fall at my feet. I've learned in public speaking it's usually best in an embarrassing moment to state the obvious so I stopped and fixed my yoke and thanked the two people who had enough sympathy for me to get my attention and resumed my welcome speech.

There is very little "our terms" in pursuing the presence of God and if we desire greater revelation and intimacy it will be on "His terms".

I adjusted the yoke to accommodate me and as a result it was unable to accomplish its intended purpose. Spiritual mountain climbing requires tremendous sacrifice and dedication and there is little room for compromise and self indulgent attitudes. There is very little "our terms" in pursuing the presence of God and if we desire greater revelation and intimacy it will be on "His terms". The life of a mountain climber demands we take His lead always even when it is difficult and we don't understand. We are not here to tell God what to do or how to be. God didn't descend all the way to the valley to meet with Moses, He came as far as the top of the mountain and called Moses up to Him. In our pursuit of God we will be tempted to call God down to us and meet us on our terms and at our convenience but He is King of the Mountain and not at our beckon call. It is our role to answer to Him and adjust to His schedule and expectations. If you want to dwell in the presence of God there will be a price to pay.

Face to Face Fellowship with the Father

In my own desire and path for deeper intimacy with God I have had to let go certain freedoms that were keeping me from the deeper walk with God. There was nothing inherently ungodly or wrong with any of them but as I pressed in they became barriers and distractions. I want to share with you five freedoms you will have to forego for face to face fellowship with the Father.

Free Time

The main ingredient for any relationship to mature is time together. For it to really grow fast it needs to be alone time. The first area God began to work with me in cultivating a relationship with Him was in my free time. The two areas for me were TV watching and sleep.

According to the A.C. Nielsen Co., the average American watches more than 4 hours of TV each day (or 28 hours/week, or 2 months of nonstop TV-watching per year). In a 65-year life, that person will have spent 9 years glued to the tube. I'm not the average American TV watcher but I do average 1-2 hours a day. I would find myself plopping down on the couch in front of the tube and immediately God would speak to my heart and say, "Turn the TV off and get in my presence." Talking about a battle of the will and breaking strong deeply rooted

Don't get caught habitually giving the networks your Prime Time and then trying to meet God during Late Night when all you really can think about is lights out.

habits. As I began to respond in obedience two things happened. My desire for TV ebbed and my anticipation of God's presence swelled. Am I advocating you chunk the 2.24 television sets A.C. Nielsen Co. says you have in your house?-- Only if God tells you to, and He might. Don't get caught habitually giving the networks your Prime Time and then trying to meet God during Late Night when all you really can think about is lights out.

I gave God permission to invite me into His presence at any time of the day or night and I would stop what I was doing and accommodate Him. He is the High King of Glory over Heaven and Earth. I figured on my terms weren't always God's terms. And He had more the right to boldly enter my presence and request my attention as He had given me access to boldly enter His presence. (Hebrews 10:19) Relationship is a two way street.

God many times picks the early hours of the morning to want to fellowship with me. It's subtle sometimes but I have learned to recognize His soft whisper and gentle touch in the serenity of the early morning hour. Some of my most pleasurable times in His presence have been before the sun peeks over the horizon. When He has me before the cares and troubles of the day have me I am more able to rest and fully enjoy His company.

I have my times set aside for God but I also anticipate and respond to the unexpected times He has set aside for me.

I have my times set aside for God but I also anticipate and respond to the unexpected times He has set aside for me.

Friends

Iron sharpens iron, so a man sharpens the face of his friend.
Proverbs 27:17

The friends in your life can be easily dichotomized: they either sharpen you or dull you. They either draw you up or pull you out. They either add wind to your sails or provide snags for your anchors. Bottom line: they help you or hurt you. Don't be deceived. There is no grey area. Let me also be clear. I am not just talking about believing friends versus unbelieving friends. In my journey to intimacy many times I have had to release Christian friends because their lukewarm, traditional, content with the status quo attitude towards God was poison to my spiritual fervor.

Chose your friends wisely.

Finances

Another area God began to work on in my journey into intimacy was where and to whom I spent my money; to be specific, my tithes and offerings. God knows how much power money can have over us. It is a pervading influence in how we make decisions. That is why God requires us to give the first of our increase. We know God doesn't need the money. Tithing first and foremost declares to ourselves and to God that He is our sustenance and all we are or can earn is because of Him. With a joyful heart we return 10% and he graciously allows us to keep the other 90%.

When I began to faithfully and consistently tithe it began to purify and influence how I spent the rest of my paycheck. On a natural level I had less to spend so the first expenditures to go were the frivolous things I didn't need to be buying in the first place. God was teaching me on all levels how to trust him in all things.

I also had a greater joy in giving. In the past there were times I tithed and in my mind I was saying, "Ouch. I feel this but I am being obedient." God honors that response. I wasn't giving ungratefully just feeling every single dollar that left my wallet. That feeling diminished and was in proportion replaced with a sincere joy and gladness in giving. What changed? God was increasing my faith in him and his Word. I trusted him with being the Financial Manager over my finances even more when my knowledge of Him increased.

Food

Do you not know that you are a temple of God, and that the Spirit of God dwells in you?

1 Corinthians 3:16

Or do you not know that your body is a temple of the Holy Spirit in you, whom you have of God? And you are not your own, for you are bought with a price. Therefore glorify God in your body and in

1 Corinthians 6:19-20

It may not sound spiritual but sometimes the most spiritual thing a person can do is take better care of their temple, or physical body.

God began to work on two areas within me: healthy eating and fasting.

Eating healthy for me was a response to having a really hard time getting up early for my morning time with God. I would set the alarm and mentally prep myself the night before. Like an Olympic athlete I would visualize myself popping out of bed when the alarm went off. Some times that was just what happened. But other times when I had the usual amount of sleep I could hardly open my eyes let alone get out of bed. I didn't understand my inconsistency.

That's when the Lord showed me on the mornings when my body felt dead to the world I had eaten a dessert or something sugary before bed. I was experiencing a sugar crash! Tweaking my diet to not eat food after 9 pm made a considerable difference in my energy level the next morning. Not eating late night desserts was a tremendous spiritual boost. I would have never discovered that knowledge reading a spiritual growth book-maybe a diet and exercise book, but not spiritual growth. God, the Holy Spirit, my Counselor and Coach told me in one of our sessions.

Fasting from food was another sacrifice God wanted from me. As I sought guidance on why the Lord began to show me some strongholds in my life that needed broken and prayer alone was not enough. These strongholds were keeping me from experiencing the depth and fullness I was seeking in the knowledge of God. These revelations for me did not come quickly. I was blind to most of them and it took the light from the Holy Spirit to illuminate my heart so I could begin the process of eradicating them from my life. It was during these times that I had to exercise the fruit of the Spirit patience and self-control.

Fasting, for me, boosted my self-control and gave me the strength I needed to overcome the exposed sins.

Future

To give God your life really means to give Him your future. It means to give Him the rest of today, tomorrow, next week, next month, next year, the next decade, to give Him every day of your not yet lived life until you die. We also measure our lives not only in days but in possessions. So to give God your life means you give him your present and future houses, cars, money, children, marriage, jobs, dreams, wants, and desires; all that you will ever have or be now and forever.

As I pressed in to God He began to show me parts of my life I was still possessing. He told me as long as I was in control there was little He was able to in those areas. Those life control issues were like buoys keeping me from launching out in to the depth of God. One of those control issues was I had failed to fully give over my plans for my future to Him.

> *God does not demand mindless lip service but faith based upon His Word that is followed up in obedience.*

One morning as I was worshipping God and enjoying His presence a sudden flash of fear gripped me. I was praying to God and expressing to Him these times with Him were priceless and meant more to me than anything. The closer I got to God the less important anything else became. In that moment of expression to God my mind thought of two deeply rooted dreams: a financially lucrative career and a godly wife. That's when I felt the fear. Would I be willing to give up both those hopes if they kept me from experiencing deeper levels of intimacy and knowledge of God? These hopes are not mutually exclusive from a relationship with God but God was testing and purifying my heart and motives. God did not want me to in the heat of the moment basking in His holiness to respond with 100% dedication and devotion and not mindfully consider what I was saying. He was reconciling my mind with my heart. God does not demand mindless lip service but faith based upon His Word that is followed up in obedience. You can not be in the presence of God and expect to remain the same.

You Can Not Stay Where You Are and Go With God

God placed before me the areas in my life I had not yet given completely over to Him. They were under the Lordship of Me not the Lordship of Christ. I could not stay where I was and go with God. A choice had to be made. As an act of my will and declaration of faith I affirmed my commitment to God and gave over my life-my entire future, and dedicated it to His service and pleasure. I gave Him my life in salvation and lost my life in service and by faith stepped in to Matthew sixteen verse twenty-five:

> *For whosoever will save his life shall lose it: and whosoever will lose his life for my sake shall find it.*
> *Matthew 16:25*

It was at that moment the fear vanished and was replaced with an overwhelming embrace of God's love. When you are honest before God He meets you where you are and lovingly draws you to Himself. He accepts you as you are but He is not content with the condition He found you in. As a loving father should, He parents you and raises you up to be a significant contributor in the Kingdom of Heaven. You are a Royal Citizen of the Kingdom of Heaven! The Great High King of Heaven has a plan and purpose for you to fulfill in His service.

His grace is free, salvation cannot be earned, but don't let those truths lull you into a spiritual sleep and miss the best part of being in Christ. Intimacy with God will cost you dearly.

There is a high price for companionship and habitation with God.

His grace is free, salvation cannot be earned, but don't let those truths lull you into a spiritual sleep and miss the best part of being in Christ. Intimacy with God will cost you dearly. It will cost you your free time, friends, finances, food, and future, and much, much more. But oh, what can compare with being a friend of God? What can compare with the surpassing greatness of knowing Christ Jesus our Lord? Is there any sacrifice too high a cost in order to dwell in His Presence, to be found righteous in Him? The Apostle Paul didn't think so:

> But whatever things were gain to me, those things I have counted as loss for the sake of Christ. More than that, I count all things to be loss in view of the surpassing value of knowing Christ Jesus my Lord, for whom I have suffered the loss of all things, and count them but rubbish so that I may gain Christ, and may be found in Him, not having a righteousness of my own derived from the Law, but that which is through faith in Christ, the righteousness which comes from God on the basis of faith, that I may know Him and the power of His resurrection and the fellowship of His sufferings, being conformed to His death; in order that I may attain to the resurrection from the dead.
>
> Philippians 3:7-11

Ascending the Mountain of God

But you have come to Mount Zion and

to the city of the living God, the heavenly Jerusalem, and

to myriads of angels,

to the general assembly and church of the firstborn who are
enrolled in heaven, and

to God, the Judge of all, and

to the spirits of the righteous made perfect, and

to Jesus, the mediator of a new covenant, and

to the sprinkled blood, which speaks better than the blood
of Abel.

See to it that you do not refuse Him who is speaking.

Hebrews 12:22-25

Mt. Zion Awaits

Mountaineers plant a flag on the peak to mark their triumph and accomplishment. Many times throughout Scripture after supernatural God-encounters, mountain peak experiences, the person would build an altar for remembrance. The first recorded account of building an altar was after the waters receded and Noah came off the ark, (Gen 8:20) Abraham build an altar to the Lord on three occasions, (Gen 12:7; 13:4; 22:9) as did Isaac and Jacob. (26:25; 33:20; 35:1-3) The altar became a visual reminder of the acts of their God for them and for their posterity. It became a place they could recount the event and be reminded of the power of their God. It stood for a place to build and rekindle the faith of the weak.

The most common "flag planting" act for me is a simple but detailed journal entry. I often return to my journal and am inspired and reminded of past God-encounters. These reminders inspire me beyond my momentary hardships or setbacks. Other "flags" or "altars of remembrance" within my journal are mementos that document the occasion. Besides written recorded entries my journal is also full of church bulletins, pictures, sermon notes, movie stubs, printed out emails and other reminders of when God revealed Himself in special and unique ways throughout my life. Take the time to write, collect and add to your spiritual journal and it will become a treasure map of your journey of faith to inspire you and even a priceless gift to pass along to your children.

From the foundation of time God has desired to dwell among his creation. That purpose was expressed in the Garden of Eden until the fall of man and sin separated Him from a Holy God. But the purpose of God cannot be denied or resisted. He tabernacled among the Israelites hovering above the mercy seat that rested on the Ark of the Covenant within the Holy of Holies. He became flesh and dwelt among men and offered His life as a ransom for sin that He might enjoy fellowship with us. After He ascended to Heaven He sent His Holy Spirit to dwell within us, to be our Guide and give us power to fulfill His will on Earth. Now as carriers of His anointing, His presence alive and active within us, we are mandated to release His anointing and presence upon a lost and dying world, to dispel the darkness and release the Light.

The more you abide in His presence the more of His presence you will be able to release. As His presence within you grows it will build to a saturate point and overflow from you to where you won't even have to tell people about Him but they will see Him in you and upon you and recognize you have been with Jesus just as the people saw Him upon Peter and John:

> *Now as they observed the confidence of Peter and John and understood that they were uneducated and untrained men, they were amazed, and began to recognize them as having been with Jesus.*
>
> Acts 4:13

But there will come a time in the last days when God will dwell among man just as He did in the Garden. The prophet Isaiah was given a glimpse of this reality in Isaiah two:

> *Now it will come about that In the last days The mountain of the house of the LORD Will be established as the chief of the mountains, And will be raised above the hills; And all the nations will stream to it. And many peoples will come and say, "Come, let us go up to the mountain of the LORD, To the house of the God of Jacob; That He may teach us*

concerning His ways And that we may walk in His paths."
For the law will go forth from Zion And the word of the
LORD from Jerusalem.

Isaiah 2:2-3

For us now Mt. Zion is a spiritual reality but our hope can be anchored to the truth that one day God's purpose will be done, He will remove the veil between the spiritual and the natural and the realities of the Kingdom of Heaven presently only visible by the eyes of faith will manifest on earth just as it is in Heaven.

In those days, when time ends and eternity begins, the Lord's Prayer will graduate from a prophetic declaration to a statement of fact: You're kingdom has come, Your will is done, on earth as it is in heaven.

Our Father who is in heaven, Hallowed be Your name.
'Your kingdom come. Your will be done, On earth as it is
in heaven.

Matthew 6:9-10

The Apostle John saw this reality in Revelation chapter 21. After the Great Tribulation when the seals were opened, the trumpets blown, and the bowls of God's judgment poured out upon mankind who persisted in their rebellion, resisted the grace of God and refused to acknowledge God as Lord and Savior (Rev. 5-20) John was shown a new heaven and a new earth and the mountain of God coming down out of heaven:

And he carried me away in the Spirit to a great and high
mountain, and showed me the holy city, Jerusalem, coming
down out of heaven from God,

Revelation 21:10

In great detail John describes the dimensions and details of the

New Jerusalem, described as a mountain coming down from the heavens. It is here that the mountain of God becomes a reality on earth as it is in Heaven. It is the culmination of the history of man that he dwell with God forever on earth. For now Heaven is a place those who die go and remain until Revelation 21 comes to pass. Then we will experience Heaven and eternity with God on a new earth and a new heaven. We will live out our eternity in the New Jerusalem, the mountain of God, the dwelling place of God where His glory will illuminate the city and there will be no need for the light of the sun or moon. That reality, of spending eternity with God forever upon Mt. Zion is what awaits those who believe. Until then we are called to bring as much of that reality to earth as we can until God completes it Himself at the end of days.

The King of the Mountain is Waiting.

Mt. Zion awaits. God calls you from His dwelling place and invites you into His presence. Answer His invitation and give Him your all and awe in worship. Come out of the valley, lay aside the weights of this world on the altar of sacrifice. Listen to His voice and move. He will meet you on the mountain and reveal Himself to you. Sit at His table and feast. Enjoy Him in fellowship. Don't let anything deter you from waiting expectantly and eagerly for Him. In His presence allow the Holy Spirit to guide and instruct you in the ways of God. When you are weary rest in Him. Let the fire of God consume you and may His zeal empower you through His Spirit to be the light this world so desperately needs. And finally, come dwell, don't let anyone or anything or any excuse keep you from His presence. The King of the mountain is waiting!

Acknowledgements

To Pastor Paula Crist:
Inspired by the prophetic anointing that flows from your
ministry, the seeds for this book were conceived and fleshed
out through a series of sermons I preached at your church.

To the people of Amen Austin! Church:
It was your faithfulness in giving, your warfare in
prayer, and encouragement to finish that gave me
the support I needed to finish this book.

To Crystal White:
It was your expert editing skills that helped turn this book
into something I could be really proud to call my own.

To my wonderful wife, Patti:
Words fail to convey my thankfulness and gratitude. You
sacrificed many an evening alone while I was hunched over
a laptop, absent to the world around me. This book never
would have been birthed without your love and support.

About the Author

M atthew White has 25 years of ministry experience. His passion is discipleship and front-line Kingdom work to advance the Gospel. He has planted two churches and founded ELITE Leadership Bible Institute, a ministry and Biblical training program whose purpose is: "Developing Leaders to Disciple the Nations." (www.elitx. org) He holds a Bachelor's in Behavioral Sciences and a Master's in Education from Concordia University. He currently is the founding pastor of Amen Austin! Church, a church in Austin, Texas (www. AmenAustin.org).

He is available for preaching, teaching, discipleship and ministry training workshops and seminars. For information, questions or comments please email pastormattwhite@gmail.com

Were you blessed by this book? Pastor Matt wants to hear from you! Send him an email or find him on Facebook at Facebook.com/ pastormattwhite.

Printed in the United States
By Bookmasters